HANDBOOK TO THE ROGUE RIVER'S HOG CREEK FLOAT

Michael L. Walker

The technical elements of this handbook focus on 25 identified riffles of which only half have previously been named. Further, it uses a refinement of the international scale of classifying riffles/rapids difficulty into six classes. The refinement is a classification that grades riffle difficulty down to one-tenth of a class. The 25 riffles on the Hog Creek float have been assigned a difficulty class rating from 0.5 to 2.2 when river temperatures are greater than 50 degrees fahrenheit.

Published and distributed by White Water Flips

Copies of this Handbook may be ordered from:

Agent
White Water Flips
850 Three Pines Road
Grants Pass, Oregon 97526
(503) 476-3019

Front Cover: Rafters Attacking Dunn Riffle
Back Cover: Orange Torpedos in Garden Riffle

Overt/Hidden Agenda: A small part of a diary for the Walker family of Hugo, Oregon

Written by Michael L. Walker
Edited by Michael L. Walker and Suzette Mecca

Computer Counseling by Mark Dyrud, The Users Corner, Medford, Oregon

Computer-generated maps and text symbols by Jacob Kent Barnett and Dave Fitzgerald of Graphic Design Services, Medford, Oregon

Illustrations and photographs by Michael L. Walker

Typesetting by Debbie Illingworth of Gandee Printing Center, Inc.

Printed in the United States of America
Gandee Printing Center, Inc.
Medford, Oregon

First Edition
ISBN 0-9621016-0-5

ACKNOWLEDGMENTS

I have been thinking for ages about writing this guide for floating this section of the Rogue River. Although I have been floating the Rogue each year since 1959, I did not seriously start writing about it until the summer of 1984. My first formal effort started when another floater and friend, Barbara Ullian, and I recorded float times on August 28, 1983. It never happened that year, but thank you Barbara.

My sister, Chris Walker, and I recorded float times again in August, 1987. We were both in my inflatable kayak (Sevytex TX 375). She was in the backseat with a waterproof clipboard. Chris also read several drafts and made suggestions for improvements. Thank you, Chris.

A good friend that floats this section in an inflatable kayak, Doug Lindsey, served as a technical consultant who reviewed drafts and offered many excellent suggestions. Thank you, Doug.

Jim Matney, another technical consultant, is a long time river guide. Jim is the owner of Otter River Trips which is a fishing and rafting company running salmon and steelhead trips all year on the Rogue River. Guided raft trips in the warm months offer fun in the water, and if one likes, you can learn to pan for gold. Thank you, Jim.

Good friends, Kit Mottice, Mary Johnson, Jan Stull, and Joyce Tripp, sharpened their pencils and told me what they thought about several drafts. Thanks women! Kit also reviewed my first galley for the purpose of reviewing the design or layout. She had some great ideas. She also salivated over the idea of using a familiar desk top publishing program. Next time Kit!

Another friend, Nancy Wright, an enthusiast of only one float on the Rogue...yes, the Hog Creek to Grave Creek run, needed to organize a float trip. Her need was another reason for my finally recording what I have been experiencing. Thank you Nancy for getting me off my butt and ending my decade of procrastination.

The enthusiasm of a fellow pinball buddy, Suzette Mecca, encouraged me to carry on a three-year research and writing path for the development of this handbook. Our strategy sessions over pinball at the "Log Cabin" of Ashland, Oregon were unusual, but stimulating. As you can see I was unable to turn back. Suzette ultimately became my writer editor. Thanks bunches, Suzette.

And finally, my best friend, Cindy Stull, has been exploring with me the exciting fantasies of the Rogue. Camping and rafting are to her like a duck shedding water. Thanks Love.

ABOUT THE AUTHOR

This author was born in California and became a world-traveling Navy brat until the sixth grade when his dad said, "Hugo, Oregon." I graduated from Hugo Elementary School, Grants Pass Junior High, Grants Pass High School and Oregon State University. I have a B.S. in Natural Resources, an M.S. in Resource Geography, and I completed all but my dissertation in a PhD. in Planning and Resource Geography. I have lived or worked in Oregon, California, Washington, Florida, Texas, Nevada, Alaska, Japan, Thailand, Viet Nam (then South), and the Philippines. My disguises have been U.S. Navy pilot; community, county, and regional planner; environmental coordinator; writer editor; environmental specialist; and now part-time writer. I have a personal passion for white water rafting and a particular love for the Hog Creek Float which I have made a summer activity since I started floating in 1959.

By Michael L. Walker

HANDBOOK TO THE ROGUE RIVER'S HOG CREEK FLOAT

TABLE OF CONTENTS

By Michael L. Walker

MAPS

TABLES

RIFFLE DIAGRAMS

By Michael L. Walker

GRAPHS

APPENDICES

The principles and concepts covered in this handbook cannot assure your safety. On the Rogue, you are responsible for your own safety. The ideas covered in this handbook are no substitute for prudence, common sense, and your own good judgment. Trust your own eyes and do not make the mistake of floating white water without knowing what you are doing.

You need to be able to read the river ahead when floating. Defensive floating includes recognizing white water hazards, understanding the defense, and acting appropriately in time.

Be cautious.

Type V Life jacket

MAP AND TEXT SYMBOLS [1]

(⟲) Riffle

(⚒) Historical Mine (lode or placer)

(☋) Indian History

(■) Historic Site/History

(▲) Improved Campground

(△) Dry Camp/Road Access

(△) Dry Camp/River Access Only

(▼) Bureau of Land Management (BLM) Recreation Site

(⌂) BLM/Forest Service Information Center

(⊼) Day-use Area

(●) Boat Landing/Ramp

(✕) Jumping Rock

(○) Osprey Nest

(△) Blue Heron Rookery

(⚘) Sensitive Plants

(☺) Sloppy Nostalgia

(↔) Distance

(🕐) Drift Time

(☀) How To

(📖) Notes

(/\ ) Tongue or "V"

(⌒⌒) Wave

(⊔) Hole or Reversal

(↻) Eddy

(⬡) Rock

(▒) Recreation Corridor Boundary

(☰) Private Property

National Wild
And Scenic
Rivers System

1. See the glossary for definitions of map symbols. **These map symbols are used on Maps 2 through 9 and in the text where** this type of information is covered.

By Michael L. Walker

HANDBOOK TO THE ROGUE RIVER'S HOG CREEK FLOAT

THANK YOU

My name is Michael L. Walker, I am the author. My friends call me "Mikie." I like to have fun! I gained my perception of the world and my pounds near Hugo, Oregon where I started floating the Rogue River in 1959 with my brothers and friends in inner-tubes. The stretch we floated on the Rogue back then was from Hog Creek to Indian Mary Park. It was a time when gas was cheap at 19 cents a gallon and we used my Dad's 1941 Chevy pickup to get there. We didn't have life vests in those days, but for the last ten years I have never taken mine off when floating, no matter how easy the water. After many, many float miles, our group, then and now, has never had a serious accident. We loved to have fun then, and still do. A float downriver and a jump off the now-destroyed old Hellgate Bridge into deep water were the highlights of the day.

I dedicate this handbook to my family and especially to my Dad and his '41 Chevy pickup. Thanks Dad!

INTRODUCTION

When you think about the Rogue River from Hog Creek to Grave Creek, you may have conflicting pictures in your mind--you may think it is either too dull, or you may think it's too exciting and therefore potentially dangerous. You're right. It can be either or both depending on your experience and attitude. My view is that the Rogue can be exciting **and** safe. The Hog Creek Float is a Class II float for white water adventurers. This handbook can be used to plan float trips for all or a portion of this stretch of the Rogue.

If you like getting outdoors, you are sure to have fun in your Class II adventure on the Rogue. All that water is yours, and the modern world of Big Macs and Whoppers seems far away. The sound of water flowing and the riparian woodland area along the river isolate you from the rest of the masses. A feeling of independence and solitude comes over you. This handbook's design is for the needs and possible interests of the inflatable kayaker and small paddle rafter. Others, hopefully, will also find this book valuable.

There are many brands of inflatable kayaks of which Sevylor's K-79 yellow Tahiti is the most well known on the Rogue. The orange version showed up in force on the Rogue in 1969 with Don Stevens founding Orange Torpedo Trips in Grants Pass, Oregon (■). The K-79 is a two-person craft about 12 feet long by 2 1/2 feet at the beam. A small paddle raft is usually classified as a six-man but good for only four people. The six-man raft is approximately 12 feet long by 5 feet at the beam. Most inflatables and small paddle rafts are thin-skinned, light weight, and cheap ($100 on sale). This type of paddle raft has been named, degradingly by some, rubber ducky because of its susceptibility for blowing up. It's true that the thin-skinned inflatable and rubber ducky do not offer the protection of the expensive heavy duty craft, but, oh! the adventure. With these smaller thin-skins you are literally "in" the river. Plus, with the ducky, all are equal to meet the challenge together. Everyone helps to propel the raft. The type of craft used makes a tremendous difference in the difficulty of a float. Your view in a ducky is not of the large heavy duty rafts (generally 13 to 16 feet long) which cover the Class I and II riffles as they cruise over them. It's a world of adventure as you disappear into a hole or crash through a standing wave coming through the riffle with more water inside your inflatable or ducky than outside. It's a loving madness.

As you start your float at the Hog Creek put-in, the elevation is 756 feet above sea level. After you complete your float at Grave Creek take-out, the elevation has dropped 144 feet over a distance of 14 miles. This 14-mile section will be referred to as the "Hog Creek Float" or the "Hog Run." The average drop per mile is ten feet, but the gradient ranges from over 26 feet per mile from the Mine Riffle to Bailey Canyon, down to six feet per mile from the end of Massie Riffle to Carpenter's Island (see Table 6). Impressive statistics, right?

There are no permits required by a floater for this section of the river unless you are a commercial guide. The Bureau of Land Management (BLM) manages this stretch of the Rogue and can provide up-to-date information (see Appendix A).

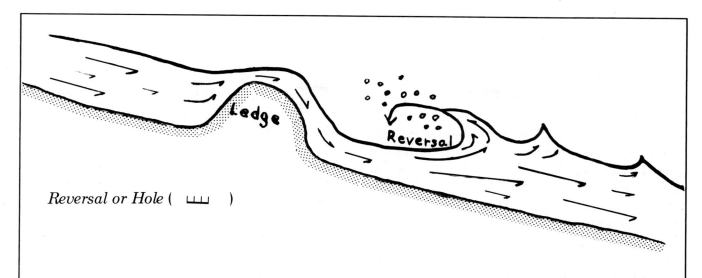

Reversal or Hole (⊔)

A reversal or hole is caused by fast water falling over a boulder or ledge which is just below the surface of the water. The water plunges to the river bottom before turning back downriver. The place where the fast current swings upward and revolves back on itself forming an exciting meeting of the currents is the hole.

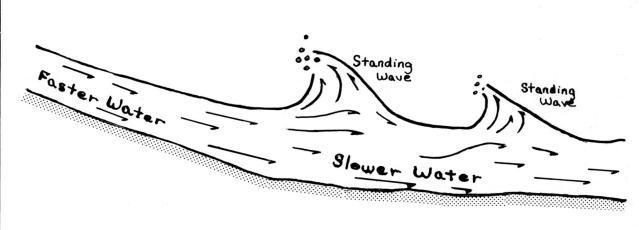

Standing Waves (ᴍ)

A standing wave is caused by the deceleration of a current that occurs when fast moving water slams into slower moving water.

By Michael L. Walker

ROGUE RIVER

Rascal Rogue (✍ ; ■)

Why is the Rogue River called the "Rogue"? History is fuzzy, especially when the white victor is the scribe. There are several stories. One story is that the name originated with the French who called the river "The Rogues" for the Indians in the area (Hill 1976). The Indians who used to live along the river were unfriendly and considered scoundrels by the whites. Stories come from as far back as 1827 which describe fur trappers lead by Jedediah S. Smith being attacked by unfriendly Indians. All but three or four of his trapping party of approximately 15 men were killed by the attacking Indians (Grants Pass Courier 1935). This conflict, and the disregard by Indians and whites (early miners) for each other's race continued through the 1850's during the time of the Indian wars. The conclusion of this tale is that the Rogue was named after the rascal or scoundrel Indians.

National Wild and Scenic River (🌀)

A portion of the Rogue River was designated in 1968 as a National Wild and Scenic River. The designated river portion was divided into management sections which were classified as wild, scenic, or recreational. This handbook deals with a 14-mile segment of a recreational section managed by the BLM from Hog Creek to Grave Creek (see Maps 1 and 2). A recreation classification applies to this section of the river because it is readily accessible by road and has some development along the shoreline (BLM 1978). A section of river with this classification is managed to provide a wide range of public outdoor recreation opportunities on the river in its free-flowing condition. Floaters of the Rogue River on this recreation section can appreciate that because of the National Wild and Scenic Rivers Act, their view from the river will be protected for generations barring natural disasters such as floods and fires. You will continue to see a natural river corridor with only occasional reminders of developments on the riverbanks. However, a word of caution to the floater: beyond the river bank, do not assume every piece of land is public land. The public lands are intermingled with private lands (see Map 2). This portion of the Rogue is also part of the Oregon State Scenic Waterways System.

The future is bright for this section of the Rogue. The BLM has instituted a planning inititative called "Recreation 2000" which outlines the agency's role in managing outdoor recreation resources for the next decade. Recreation 2000 provides a positive and proactive direction for recreation management. It directs the BLM to enhance and protect the resource, manage through partnerships with different user groups, and act as a leading force in the promotion of outdoor recreation.

The BLM has proposed some improvements and additions to the recreation developments that exist on the river. Should funding become available, visitors to the Rogue will be able to enjoy improved river access, camping facilities, launch facilities and river information services. The agency appears eager to pursue an expanded role in recreation resource management. The opportunities for expansion and new developments exist now. Through careful planning efforts, perhaps the Rogue's beauty can become more available to the public for generations to come.

By Michael L. Walker

MAP 1
ROAD TRIP AND SHUTTLE

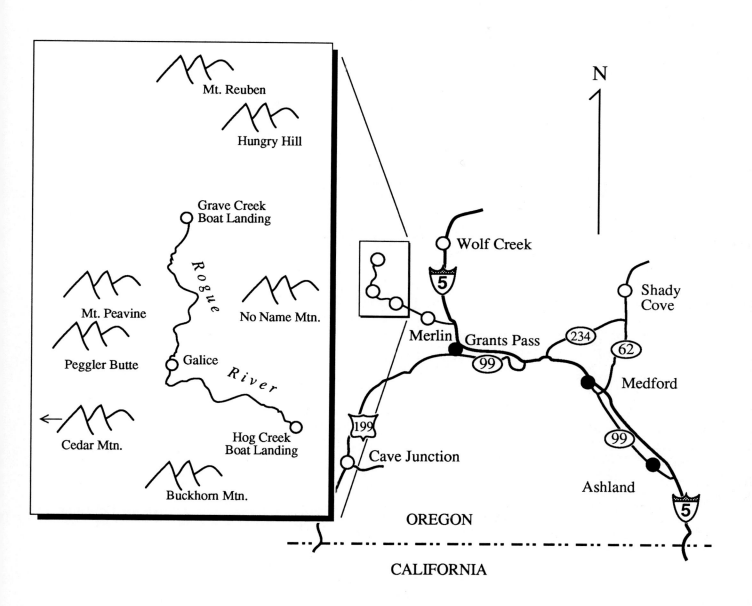

Scale: 0 5 10   20   30 Miles

See Table 3 for more information.

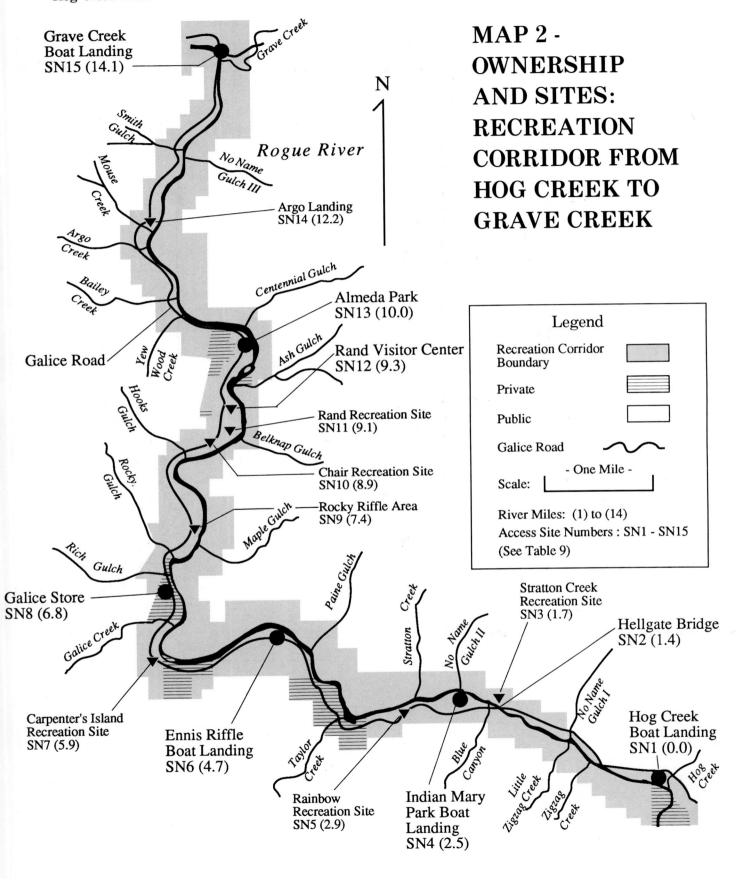

Grave Creek
Boat Landing
SN15 (14.1)

Grave Creek

Smith
Gulch

Rogue River

No Name
Gulch III

Mouse
Creek

Argo Landing
SN14 (12.2)

Argo
Creek

Bailey
Creek

Centennial Gulch

Almeda Park
SN13 (10.0)

Galice Road

Yew
Wood Creek

Ash Gulch

Rand Visitor Center
SN12 (9.3)

Hooks
Gulch

Rand Recreation Site
SN11 (9.1)

Belknap Gulch

Rocky
Gulch

Chair Recreation Site
SN10 (8.9)

Rocky Riffle Area
SN9 (7.4)

Maple Gulch

Rich
Gulch

Galice Store
SN8 (6.8)

Galice Creek

Paine Gulch

Stratton
Creek

Stratton Creek
Recreation Site
SN3 (1.7)

Hellgate Bridge
SN2 (1.4)

No Name
Gulch II

No Name
Gulch I

Hog Creek
Boat Landing
SN1 (0.0)

Hog
Creek

Carpenter's Island
Recreation Site
SN7 (5.9)

Ennis Riffle
Boat Landing
SN6 (4.7)

Taylor
Creek

Rainbow
Recreation Site
SN5 (2.9)

Blue
Canyon

Indian Mary
Park Boat
Landing
SN4 (2.5)

Little
Zigzag Creek

Zigzag
Creek

MAP 2 - OWNERSHIP AND SITES: RECREATION CORRIDOR FROM HOG CREEK TO GRAVE CREEK

Legend

Recreation Corridor
Boundary

Private

Public

Galice Road

- One Mile -

Scale:

River Miles: (1) to (14)
Access Site Numbers : SN1 - SN15
(See Table 9)

By Michael L. Walker

Management Zones Within The Recreation Section

There are several types of management zones within this 14-mile recreation corridor. The floating public can stop on most of the shoreline in this section of the river without fear of trespass as the Bureau of Land Management has acquired an easement on most private property to permit the public to walk on a ten-foot wide strip of land along the water's edge. This easement does not give the public the right to cross private property to reach the river. Only two major management zones will be considered herein: the natural and open space zones.

Natural Zone

The right bank downriver from the Stratton Creek Recreation Site to Grave Creek and the left bank downriver from Yew Wood Creek (below Almeda Park) to Grave Creek are managed by the BLM as a natural zone (see Map 2). This zone is managed as a transition zone between the primitive conditions of the wild section of the Rogue downriver from Grave Creek and the more developed land upriver (BLM 1978). In fact, your view of the river and land from the Galice Road into the natural zone is essentially the same visual experience you would get if you were in the wild section. No developments visible from the river are permitted in the natural zone. Except for one parcel, all of the land in the natural zone is public land. The BLM land is open for overnight camping, although no facilities are provided. The private parcel is on the right bank between Rand and Widow Maker Riffle. It can be located by looking for a power line passing over your head as you drift by Ash Gulch.

In 1985, a party of 11 and I had the delightful occasion to make dry camp at river mile 2.8 for three days. The camp site was a small sandy beach next to Stratton Creek (below Indian Mary Park) in the natural zone. You

Dry Camp (△) Next to Stratton Creek, River Mile 2.8

By Michael L. Walker

can legally camp up to 14 consecutive days at all of the dry camp sites accessible only by river. [Look on the maps for the river dry camp site symbol (△). If it is hot and dry you should check with the Oregon State Department of Forestry prior to building a camp fire (see Appendix A)]. No permits were required, we just had to get the camp site first. Starting at the Merlin-Galice Road our party ferried our camping gear across the river above Massie Riffle in inflatable kayaks. Each day we would float the Rogue downriver to Grave Creek. So close to nature and so far from the "real world." The land and river were ours for three whole days. HOORAYYYYY!

Open Space Zone

The majority of the rest of this recreation corridor is managed as an open space zone. This zone is generally in public ownership interspersed with private land. The public lands are managed to enhance natural values. Day-use activities are emphasized with camping encouraged at developed facilities with improved campgrounds.

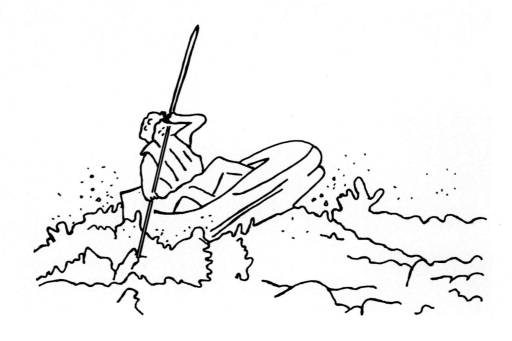

By Michael L. Walker

HISTORY

Mining (⛏)

The area is rich in mining history. The gold rush began in the Galice area in 1851, and with it came the white settlement of the Rogue River Canyon. The Galice area was significant in southwest Oregon with the production of millions of dollars in gold. The Old Channel Mine is close to Galice and was one of the largest hydraulic mining operations in the United States (Grants Pass Courier 1935; Oregon 1952; Armstead and Schultz 1904). Most of the lode gold deposits are in quartz-fissure veins. Quartz mining for gold started during the mid-1880's with the major mining efforts ending during World War II. Some of the major quartz mines in the Galice area along this portion of the Rogue were the Almeda, Black Bear, Gold Plate, Golden Wedge, Hansen, Oriole, Seven-Thirty, Sugar Pine, and Victor mines (see Table 1). The very names spell excitement and the mystery of the past. Evidence of mining still remains and includes piles of rocks along stream banks, some tunnels, and rusting equipment in areas hydraulically mined.

Much of the area was hydraulically mined for gold, but many a pioneer miner was of the shovel, pick, and pan type. Sweat and brawn was the name of the game. Small nuggets are still found today. Find three pennyweights of gold and pay for your day's outing. Let's go gold mining! The most popular types of recreational gold mining include panning and dredging. Recreational gold panning is permitted on most of the unclaimed public lands within the recreation corridor if it does not require digging, dredging, or sluicing (USDI 1981; see Map 2). Recreational gold dredging is allowed in accordance with Oregon State law and regulations with up to a three-inch diameter motorized suction dredge in the river channel (BLM 1981). The river channel is defined as the area of the river that is underwater when the river level is at mean high water. The controlled dredging season is from June 15th through August 31st each year. Skin diving for gold in the murky depths of the Rogue is also popular. The ever-present possibility that there may be gold at the next spot drives us on. Individual sniping for gold is the way!

Indian Wars (🖋)

I cannot state that the Indian history is weightier than the mining history, but together they are powerful. There were a series of battles between the Rogue Indians and the white settlers in Josephine County during the major war of 1855-1856. Josephine County was actually formed from a portion of Jackson County in 1856. War between the Indians and the whites broke out in 1855, four years prior to Oregon being admitted to the Union in 1859. One major battle of this war, the "Siege of Galice," was fought at Skull Bar near the site of the present Galice Store (Hill 1976). The town of Galiceburg, which was near the mouth of Galice Creek, was destroyed. White settlers were saved at Skull Bar only by a warning from a local Indian named Umpqua Joe who was seriously injured in the fighting.

The war lasted a couple of years and was essentially over when the last major Indian chief surrendered in 1856. After the Indian wars were over, Umpqua Joe and his family were allowed to stay in the Rogue Valley while the other local Indians were sent to the Siletz Indian Reservation. The first 10 years at the reservation have been described as deadly: "...climate, poor diets, poor sanitation, fighting, and lung disease contracted during the war, killed 205 of them the first year, cutting their population from 590 to 385. By 1865, there were only 121 of them left. Thus came the downfall of a proud people" (Kent 1973).

By Michael L. Walker

Umpqua Joe died in a gun fight with his daughter's husband, Albert Peco (Booth 1975). Later in 1885, the government of the United States gave his daughter, Mary, a grant to the home and land she occupied on the Rogue. It was known as the "smallest reservation ever created." In 1896 Mary rented the reservation and moved to Grants Pass, Oregon (Grants Pass Courier 1935). Later a county park, Indian Mary Park, was named after Mary and was developed at the location of her old home site.

A small, but hardy survivor of the Indian Wars is an old apple tree in Merlin, Oregon. It was long ago fenced off and represents the last visual evidence of the Haines' homestead. A Josephine County Historical Site marker near the apple tree reads,

> *"Homestead where the Haines family were massacred. Mr. Haines was found murdered and scalped. His young sons were killed with tomahawks. Mrs. Haines and a daughter were taken captive. Later killed and their bodies thrown into the Rogue River near Hellgate. Volunteer militia found this horrible scene duplicated many times in the Rogue River valley on that tragic day October 9, 1855."*

Floods (■)

Floods on the Rogue prior to the building of Lost Creek Dam have continually claimed their due by sweeping away homes and other structures (see Table 2; Hill 1976). The angry brown of tons of water carrying its burden to the Pacific blue is the description of any flood, but especially describes the biggest one ever officially recorded in 1964 (Sutton 1966). Think of how high and wide the present Hellgate Bridge is to get an idea of how much water tore down the Rogue during the 1964 flood. This present-day bridge is 765 feet long and was designed to be higher than the flood waters which were 152,000 cubic feet per second (cfs) at Grants Pass, Oregon. The bottom of the bridge is approximately 70 feet above the average summer flow level and would probably be 5 to 10 feet above this highest recorded flood level. For comparison, 2,269 cfs was the average monthly flow at Grants Pass during June, July, and August of 1985.

Area Today

The area within the recreation corridor of the "Hog Run" is today a collection of a few residential homes; local fishing, rafting, and tourist businesses; public parks and other recreation amenities; miners; and rural living, all of which are tied to the Merlin-Galice Road like popcorn on a string. The area still has a flavor of local independence inherited from the past. However, the red-neck miner, die-hard fisherman, and local resident population is largely a winter scene as the summer finds the area invaded by hordes of pleasure seekers floating the Rogue.

By Michael L. Walker

ACCESS

Geography

This 14-mile recreational section of the Rogue River is surrounded by steep rugged mountains (see Map 1). Buckhorn Mountain topping out at 3,736 feet dominates the south end of this recreational section of the Rogue. The western fence is formed by Cedar Mountain at 4,305 feet, Peggler Butte, and Mt. Peavine at 4,305 feet. The east finds a mountain complex with no name reaching an elevation of approximately 3,500 feet. Hungry Hill at 3,682 feet and Mount Reuben climbing to 4,016 feet form the northern wall which, together with the other mountains, effectively surround this area of Josephine County. There is a story about a volunteer soldier who fought in the Rogue Indian Wars whose name was Reuben (⚜). As the story goes, his company was preparing to cross the Rogue when he joked about the Indians making an attack. Apparently they did and the local road, Mount Reuben Road, was named after the event.

Importance of Rogue River

Limited access to the narrow Rogue plain is provided by the river itself, the major artery of the geography of the entire southern Oregon drainage, and the natural paths along a few major tributaries. A sign near a boat display at the Bureau of Land Management/Forest Service Visitors Center (🏠) in Rand testifies to the importance of the river (■).

"Early River Transportation Trip down Rogue River: The gold rush of the 1850's brought settlement to the Rogue River Canyon. Supplies were brought in primarily by pack train, but packing was exhausting, time consuming, and expensive."

"Early attempts to navigate the Rogue were often disastrous but increasing demand for larger, bulky mining equipment, stoves, and pianos encouraged blasting of impassable rapids and improvements of white water crafts."

"The boat in front of you was recently salvaged intact from the Rogue River Ranch at Marial. It was built and used on the Rogue River in the 1930's. Because of the difficulty in returning a boat upstream, boats similar to this one were often disassembled and used for lumber after one trip downstream."

Go see this boat!

By Michael L. Walker

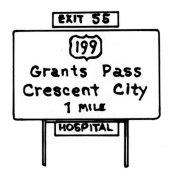

Grants Pass/Merlin

Today, access to this part of the Rogue is usually gained through the city of Grants Pass and through the community of Merlin, Oregon on the Merlin-Galice Road, a wide, paved, scenic, two-lane highway (see Map 1, Sutton 1966). This road in the Galice area was at one time called the Galice Windy Gap State Highway. Grants Pass was named in honor of General Grant in 1865 when the city was incorporated. If you are from out of town, it will probably be your home base for most of your rafting excursions on the Rogue.

Merlin is seven miles from Grants Pass. Just prior to arriving in Merlin you will pass the Miller Redwood Company. The Bate Mill Wigwam Burner is at the rear of their property. It is one of three wigwam burners still standing in northern Josephine County (Atwood 1984).

Merlin came into existence in the 1880's as a railroad station. Merlin was named by a railroad employee, Mr. David Loring, in 1882 for the merlins that were in the neighborhood (Murphy 1988). These birds are known locally as pigeon hawks. The Merlin Post Office was established in 1886 (Sutton 1966).

Merlin has several historic structures (■), three of which are: the former Merlin General Store, the Merlin Post Office, and the Southern Pacific Depot for Merlin. The Merlin General Store is today known as the Merlin Mining Company. It was built in 1904 and is one of a few buildings which survived a disastrous fire near the turn of the century. It was constructed for use as a general mercantile company. It has been used as a community center, a grange, and now as a restaurant. Don't miss the dinner theatre at the Blue Heron Opera House which is also at the Merlin Mining Company!

The second Merlin Post Office was constructed in 1934, replacing the earlier office called McAllister. It was used as a post office until 1967 when the current post office was constructed. Today, the old post office is being used as a private residence, but remains little changed. It is located on the southwest corner of the intersection of Merlin Avenue and Stratton Street.

By Michael L. Walker

The former Southern Pacific Railroad Depot is today known as the Merlin Trading Post. It has had many alterations over the years, but the core of the old depot remains intact and quite recognizable. The depot was originally built in 1883 for Grants Pass and was moved to serve in Merlin in 1897. The building adds significance to the area and Josephine County as a whole (Atwood 1984).

The community has several grocery stores. I like the "Lil Pantry." Mike Chanquet, the owner, is a swell guy. There is also a great rural restaurant, "Buzz's," for eating breakfast.

A watering hole goes by the name "Merlin Pizza, White Water Saloon." I love it! The owners of the saloon, Irving and Karen Baldini, are an interesting and knowledgeable couple who will be happy to tell you all about the area.

By Michael L. Walker

13

WHITE WATER COWBOYS

Local color comes with Jim Chanquet's White Water Cowboys. The Cowboys are a local rafting business that should be able to satisfy any of your needs from the rental of a single paddle to the outfitting of a large party running the wild section on a three-day trip.

If you have been there before, gustatory memories of baked breads and pastries will cause you to see if "The Cake Shop" is open. Check the flow as you're leaving town on the river conditions board of Ralph Graham's bait and tackle shop, "Skipper's Fishing Tackle." The "Hideaway" is a local restaurant west of Merlin that offers good food. After you leave Merlin, you still have six miles to the put-in at Hog Creek down the Merlin-Galice Road, and a 30-mile round trip shuttle to Grave Creek and back to the put-in (see Table 3).

The Merlin-Galice Road, hereafter called the Galice Road, was always rough and narrow prior to the most recent road construction in the 50's and 60's. As a youngster I can remember traveling to the river to go fishing with my father on a narrow, winding, gravel road. The drive to a favorite fishing hole was an ordeal. Many homes and developments have been obliterated by the Galice Road as it has grown and changed into its present form.

By Michael L. Walker

THE FLOAT: HOG CREEK TO GRAVE CREEK

Welcome to the "Disneyland Float," or the "Hog Run," where you'll find lots of floaters, fun, and excitement! The majority of the floaters of the Disneyland Float drift during the warm and dry summer months.

The format for this guide is to enjoy it river-section-by-river-section as it relates to major boat landing access sites. There are five such sections:

• Hog Creek Boat Landing to Indian Mary Park Boat Landing - 2.5 river miles,

• Indian Mary Park Boat Landing to Ennis Riffle Boat Landing - 2.2 river miles,

• Ennis Riffle Boat Landing to Galice Store Boat Landing - 2.1 river miles,

• Galice Store Boat Landing to Almeda Park Boat Landing - 3.2 river miles, and

• Almeda Park Boat Landing to Grave Creek Boat Landing - 4.1 river miles.

Total: 14.1 river miles.

It is estimated that the total float time it takes to travel the 14.1 river miles, between put-in and take-out, varies between six and seven hours (see Table 3). River floating time is affected by many factors: wind, type of craft, and river flow. River flow will vary as influenced by water releases from the Lost Creek and Applegate dams. In the summer it normally varies from 1,500 cubic feet per second (cfs) to around 2,400 cfs (see Tables 4 and 5). Winds are generally not severe. However, sometimes afternoon upriver winds can slow your progress and make your float a form of work.

Remember that left and right bank are as viewed when looking downriver. The "How To" sections in this handbook are also from this viewpoint. The "How To" sections describe the riffles, obstructions, and recommendations for how to float the riffles.

Most of the river valley is narrow and steep on this section of the Rogue with Douglas-fir, pine, oak, manzanita, poison oak, and madrone covering the mountains. There is some residential development on the left bank, but the right bank is essentially in its natural state.

Each river section is covered by a chapter with a map at the beginning. Each chapter is divided into major points of interest, usually white water action points or access, with the river miles identified. Water action points or riffles have a difficulty class rating assigned from 0.5 to 2.2 based on a six-point system (see Map 3, Table 6, Graph 2, and Appendix B). The rating in this guide is based on a "ducky" or inflatable running the wildest route of the riffles possible at a flow ranging from 2,000 cfs to 2,300 cfs at Grants Pass. As far as I know I'm the only one to date with the audacity to assign a difficulty rating down to one-tenth of a class.

How to run the riffles, my sloppy nostalgia, and local history are also included in the type of information covered. There is a glossary of terms at the back of this handbook. The river mile at the Hog Creek put-in is 0.0 increasing as one floats downriver until one reaches the end of the run at the Grave Creek Boat Landing take-out at river mile 14.1 (see Appendix H).

This Class II float is not about safety, but never forget about it (see Table 8; Appendix D)! You be cool on the water, be smart, and float the Rogue many more times.

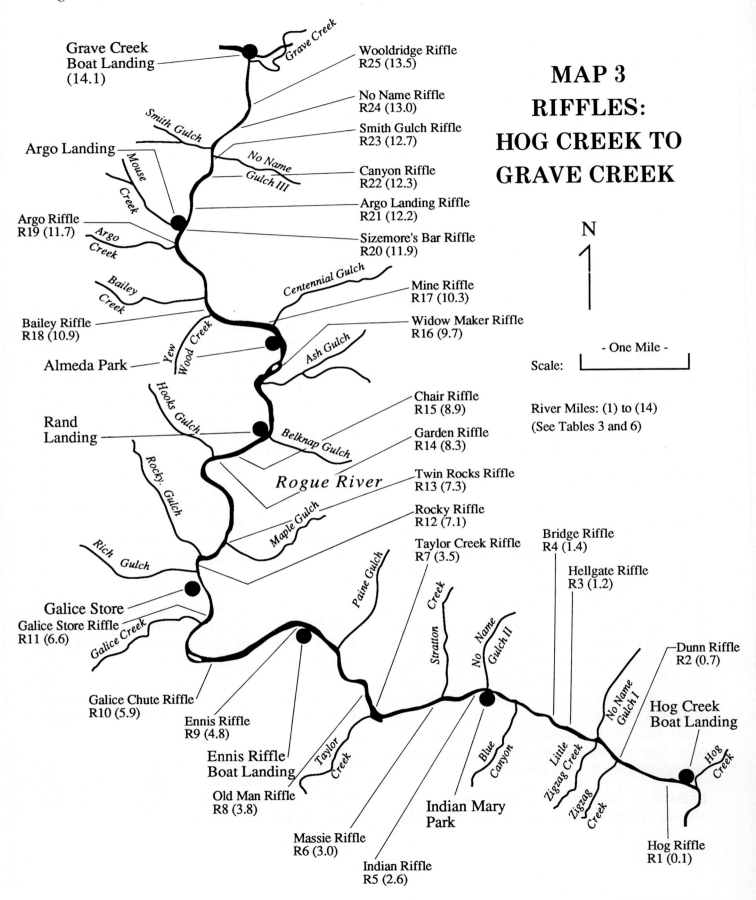

Grave Creek
Boat Landing
(14.1)

Wooldridge Riffle
R25 (13.5)

No Name Riffle
R24 (13.0)

Smith Gulch Riffle
R23 (12.7)

Canyon Riffle
R22 (12.3)

Argo Landing

Argo Landing Riffle
R21 (12.2)

Sizemore's Bar Riffle
R20 (11.9)

Argo Riffle
R19 (11.7)

Bailey Riffle
R18 (10.9)

Mine Riffle
R17 (10.3)

Widow Maker Riffle
R16 (9.7)

Almeda Park

Chair Riffle
R15 (8.9)

Rand
Landing

Garden Riffle
R14 (8.3)

Rogue River

Twin Rocks Riffle
R13 (7.3)

Rocky Riffle
R12 (7.1)

Taylor Creek Riffle
R7 (3.5)

Bridge Riffle
R4 (1.4)

Hellgate Riffle
R3 (1.2)

Galice Store

Galice Store Riffle
R11 (6.6)

Dunn Riffle
R2 (0.7)

Hog Creek
Boat Landing

Galice Chute Riffle
R10 (5.9)

Ennis Riffle
R9 (4.8)

Ennis Riffle
Boat Landing

Old Man Riffle
R8 (3.8)

Indian Mary
Park

Hog Riffle
R1 (0.1)

Massie Riffle
R6 (3.0)

Indian Riffle
R5 (2.6)

MAP 3
RIFFLES:
HOG CREEK TO
GRAVE CREEK

N

- One Mile -

Scale:

River Miles: (1) to (14)
(See Tables 3 and 6)

Smith Gulch

Mouse Creek

No Name Gulch III

Argo Creek

Bailey Creek

Centennial Gulch

Yew Wood Creek

Ash Gulch

Hooks Gulch

Belknap Gulch

Rocky Gulch

Maple Gulch

Rich Gulch

Paine Gulch

Stratton Creek

No Name Gulch II

Galice Creek

Taylor Creek

Blue Canyon

Little Zigzag Creek

Zigzag Creek

No Name Gulch I

Hog Creek

By Michael L. Walker

The "Clan" at Hog Creek Put-in, River Mile 0.0

Floaters Patiently Waiting for Their Shuttle Driver(s) at Put-in: River Mile 0.0

By Michael L. Walker

HOG CREEK BOAT LANDING TO INDIAN MARY PARK BOAT LANDING

Refer to the map entitled "Hog Creek Boat Landing to Indian Mary Park Boat Landing" for a geographic description of the major points of float interest (see Map 4). This river stretch has a white water (WW) index of WW 0.4. The white water index is a measure of the floating difficulty of a river segment or stretch (see Appendix B).

0.0 RIVER MILE, HOG CREEK BOAT LANDING

One of the greatest things about floating is that no matter who you are, or what your socioeconomic background, or your sex or age, you will find brothers and sisters in love with the same adventure who will not only empathize with you but will want to know more about you. You belong to a pretty impressive group. Trust them--your fellow floaters can become friends.

Hog Creek Boat Landing Description (●)

Hog Creek enters the Rogue on the right bank just upriver from the Josephine County Hog Creek Boat Landing (see Map 4). The landing itself is upriver from Hellgate Canyon. It is the start of your float trip. There is a paved road leading to a concrete boat launch area. Here is where your inflatable kayak or rubber ducky demands air, with you continually monitoring how much air. The squeeze test works well, but when the craft is placed in the cold water, it suddenly needs more air.

As you wait for your shuttle people to return, you mentally pre-flight your adventure and go over the items you wanted to bring but forgot:

- inflatable (no holes)
- air pump (big, it's easier pumping)
- life vest (it fits)
- paddle (no cracks)
- pants (right color)
- dry bag (no holes)
- lunch (peanut butter)
- beer (your favorite brewski)
- sun tan screen (nose job)
- tennis shoes (with laces)
- friend (right sex)
- shuttle rig (at take-out)
- patch kit (with glue)
- first-aid kit (for morale)
- dry clothes (in your rig)
- hot day (maybe prayers)
- water fight bucket (bigger than the buckets of the people you attack)
- keys for your shuttle rig (hidden where you can find them)
- water proof camera (for silly memories)
- river maps (hopefully laminated with plastic)

By Michael L. Walker

MAP 4
HOG CREEK BOAT LANDING TO
INDIAN MARY PARK BOAT LANDING

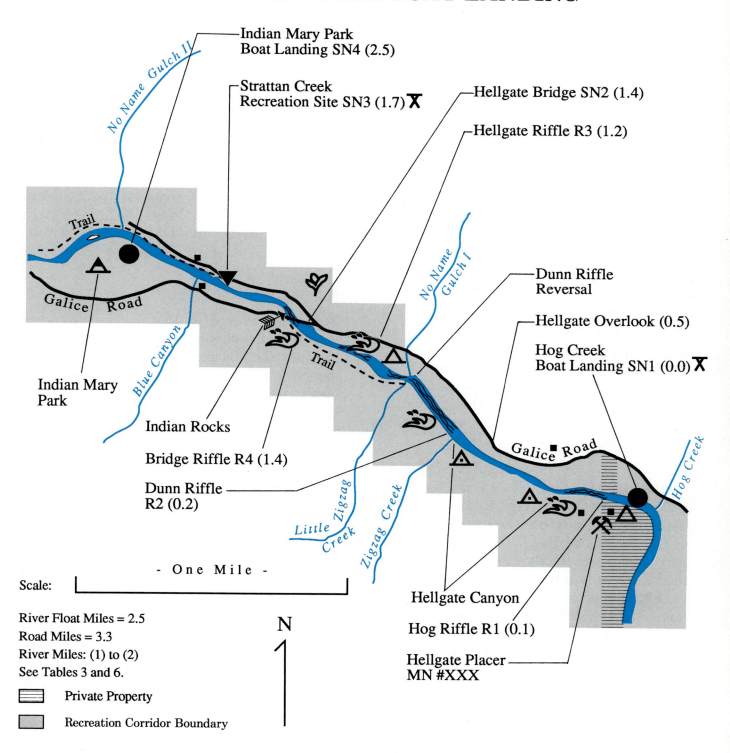

Indian Mary Park
Boat Landing SN4 (2.5)

Strattan Creek
Recreation Site SN3 (1.7)

Hellgate Bridge SN2 (1.4)

Hellgate Riffle R3 (1.2)

No Name Gulch II

No Name Gulch I

Trail

Galice Road

Blue Canyon

Indian Mary
Park

Indian Rocks

Bridge Riffle R4 (1.4)

Dunn Riffle
R2 (0.2)

Little Zigzag Creek

Zigzag Creek

Trail

Dunn Riffle
Reversal

Hellgate Overlook (0.5)

Hog Creek
Boat Landing SN1 (0.0)

Galice Road

Hog Creek

Hellgate Canyon

Hog Riffle R1 (0.1)

Hellgate Placer
MN #XXX

Scale:

- One Mile -

River Float Miles = 2.5
Road Miles = 3.3
River Miles: (1) to (2)
See Tables 3 and 6.

N

Private Property

Recreation Corridor Boundary

There is also time to check out the many different outfits (i.e., drift boats, heavy duty oar and paddle rafts, and our duckies and inflatables). Feeling friendly you can compliment other floaters on their sharp looking outfits. Strangers here are only friends you haven't met yet.

Facilities (X)

This day-use area has toilets and a parking area accommodating about 15 vehicles at the boat ramp area, with room up the hill and off-site for another 25 to 30 vehicles. The uphill parking area is nice and you are encouraged to use it and avoid congesting the boat ramp area. A well-maintained trail goes from the south end of the parking area along Hog Creek to the ramp area.

Drift Distance (←→) /Time (🕐) To Indian Mary Park Boat Landing - 2.5 miles/ 3/4 to 1 hour

History (■)

The left bank of the Rogue once was hydraulically mined (across from the mouth of Hog Creek high above the river flow) (Grants Pass Courier 1935). It was known as the Hellgate Placer Mine of Wells. Today the excavations of the placer mine can still be seen from the Galice Road.

Take off the main Galice Road one drive-way north of the Hog Creek Boat Landing exit for a glimpse of what transportation was like in the Galice area as late as the 1950's. A remnant of the old Galice Road is resplendent in its narrow one-way, winding, gravel design. The road dead-ends into the base of the present Galice Road after about one-quarter mile, but it is still passable for two-wheel drive vehicles. It has several fishermen access trails from it to the upper part of Hellgate Canyon.

Notes (📖)

There is a small great blue heron rookery (△) in the Cottonwood across the river from the boat landing. The great blue heron is a wading bird with long legs, neck, and bill. If it is not frightened, it will stay statue-like as you drift by. When alarmed it will probably fly away and emit a series of four hoarse squawks. It is graceful and wondrous in flight with a wingspan of four to five feet!

Are you ready? LET'S DO IT!

0.1 RIVER MILE, HOG RIFFLE

Riffle Class and Length (🛶)

Hog Riffle (#1) is your first riffle having a difficulty of Class I (0.6) with a drift distance of approximately 400 yards. All the 25 identified riffles on the Hog Creek Float have a class rating of I or II followed by a classification down to one-tenth of a class (see Appendix B).

How To (💡)

This is an easy riffle that starts soon after your launch and ends right after you make it through the Hellgate Canyon entrance. Follow several "V's." "V's" are smooth tongues of fast water found at the head of riffles where the river channel narrows, or areas of riffles where there is a distinct gradient drop. Your first "V" is just 100 yards downriver of the boat ramp. Miss the rock to the left. You should be ready to float left of midriver 100 yards above the canyon entrance. There is a good standing wave here at lower summer flow levels. Just remember to bear hard left to make the "jaws" (canyon entrance) which will miss the water sweeping into the "sentinel rock" (a house-sized rock which is right bank and part of the jaws). There is a strong eddy and turbulence behind this rock. Safety is paramount, not because of the type of riffle, but to avoid complacency. Several people have died here. They were not wearing life vests (see Table 8). The river immediately pools up after sentinel rock.

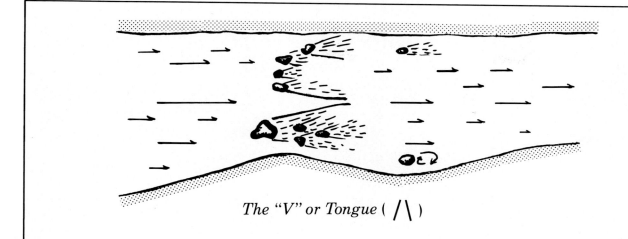

The "V" or Tongue (/\ )

The largest "V" shaped tongue of smooth water above a riffle usually marks the path of the main current, and the best point of entry.

0.2 RIVER MILE, HELLGATE CANYON

Description

When the Rogue River is flooding, the boiling and churning of the water in the canyon is dramatic, presumably like that of the gate to hell. I was standing on the cliff just above sentinel rock in March, 1989 when the river flow was about 11,000 cfs. The entrance to the canyon reminded me of a Class IV rapid in the wild section of the Rogue called Mule Creek Canyon. There were no huge rapids, but the boils and undertows looked like the "Coffee Pot."

Hellgate Canyon is narrow because the rock here is a type of volcanic rock which resists erosion. It is approximately 700 yards in length. In one place in the canyon the depth of the water was measured at 104 feet by stunt men during the filming of the movie *Rooster Cogburn* starring John Wayne and Kathryn Hepburn. I can remember when the filming occurred. I still have a T-shirt which has "Rooster Cogburn"

sprayed on it. The "FBI Story," "Gunsmoke," "Route 66," and "Vegas" were TV shows which also had scenes filmed within the canyon.

You can kick back and enjoy the views in the canyon, as there are no riffles within it. There is an easy peaceful feeling about being so small and alone within the craggy, steep, grey and white canyon walls. The flow of the blue water (sometimes grey-blue) in the canyon is usually slow. There is a small sandy beach on the left side of the river as you enter the canyon. It's a dry camp (△).

Sloppy Nostalgia (☺)

Once in the canyon a few hundred yards after passing through the "jaws," I had one of those random boils suck down the six-man paddle raft I was in. Silence replaced the water fight we'd started. It felt like a river god had glue on his hand which he stuck to the bottom of my raft while he lowered it into the depths of the river. The water was just coming over the side of the raft when the glue broke loose. I felt better about 10 minutes later.

The "Jaws" at the Entrance to Hellgate Canyon, River Mile 0.2

History (■)

There once was an early-day aerial cable car above the entrance to the canyon which was used to transport miners and goods across the Rogue to the Hellgate placer mining operation (Murphy 1988).

Notes ( )

Intriguing rock formations carved by the flowing water, some with gourd-like jugs of mud attached to them, are found within the canyon. These jugs are the nests of cliff swallows. The cliff swallows winter in South America each year and are of the same type that arrive each year at the San Juan Capistrano Mission in California.

This is a great place for a water fight. Your bailer works well for this purpose. Fill it up with water, hide it in your inflatable or ducky, and then...wait.

It is also a good time to practice bracing if you're new to inflatables and happen to be in one. Practice makes perfect because the marriage between a new inflatable runner and the craft may not be made in heaven (see river mile 14.1, Sloppy Nostalgia). Bracing is a maneuver by which a hardshell kayaker or inflatable kayaker steadies his boat with a paddle to prevent a flip. If you are flipping you do not go to the high side, a technique which will save you in a ducky. What you should do is paddle charge the water on the low side which forces the low tube of the inflatable back up to a stable position.

By Michael L. Walker

0.5 RIVER MILE, HELLGATE CANYON OVERLOOK (■)

When you get to the end of the canyon you are now adjacent to the Hellgate Canyon overlook which is on the right bank and up approximately 170 feet.

The Hellgate Canyon Landmark is located at the overlook. It is a bronze plaque mounted on a concrete base. The plaque reads:

> *"Hellgate Canyon of Rogue River 1971. That the grandeur and natural beauty of Hellgate Canyon may ever delight the people of Oregon, Pacific Power and Light Company dedicates these surrounding lands along the Rogue River as a part of the Wild and Scenic Rivers system. Glenn L. Jackson, Chairman of the Board for Pacific Power and Light Company. Roger C. B. Morton, Secretary of the Interior of the United States."*

The Galice Road is established as one of the most scenic routes in Josephine County and the canyon is one of the most scenic spots on the river. The view from the overlook is unparalleled. There is a trail from the overlook taking you to a rock overlooking the canyon. If you are a Sunday pleasure driver bring your camera. Zigzag Creek enters the Rogue here on the left bank. The canyon opens at this point with small sandy beaches on both sides of the river. There is a small amount of flat water prior to the approach of Dunn Riffle.

Inflatable Kayakers in Dunn Riffle, River Mile 1.0

By Michael L. Walker

0.7 RIVER MILE, DUNN RIFFLE

Riffle Class and Length ( )

Dunn Riffle (#2) is a Class II (2.2) riffle when the floater hits the major reversal. The drift distance is approximately 500 yards.

How To ( )

Dunn Riffle regularly flips inflatables and small paddle rafts. Therefore, I will help you with a few tips. The approach to upper Dunn is through the "V" between car-size rocks on the right and sleeper rocks (submerged at high water) on the left. The "V" usually indicates the safest passage through any rocks. The water starts to move rapidly at this point. Your approach should remain midriver. A dense wall of olive green willows guards the right bank.

At about two hundred yards downriver from the entrance tongue is a sleeper rock just to port if you have maintained midriver. It is just prior to this point (next to a small beach on the left bank) that a floater should be maneuvering for his desired approach to the major white water ahead. The small eddy next to the beach is a good spot to put in and scout the reversal. The last 75 yards prior to the fault zone has several submerged rocks in all approaches. There are three routes, depending on the floater's goals: a) close left bank approach is the least difficult, as you can sneak around the difficult spots; b) next in difficulty is the broken "V" slightly to the right of midriver; and c) the wildest section of the riffle which is the reversal left of river center. You will not see Little Zigzag Creek while floating since you will be too busy, but it enters the river on the left bank.

The reversal is created by a fault crossing the river bottom at a perpendicular angle to the river flow. The recommended approach to the left avoids the major fault drop-zone. The broken "V" approach impacts a good drop with large standing waves. The left-of-center approach impacts a major standing wave/ reversal. Inflatables: be prepared to Brace! Brace! Brace! Right of "V" has submerged rocks and is not recommended. As the water falls off your eyes you should maintain midriver position for the rest of the run and enjoy several more waves (see Diagram 1 and Appendix C). The river widens at the end of the riffle. There is a large, easy, eddy right bank to catch and bail while remembering the run. It also can be used to eddy upriver to run the lower part of Dunn Riffle again and again. A sandy beach on right bank is a nice place to reorganize as necessary. In my opinion this is one of the best overall riffles of the entire 14-mile float.

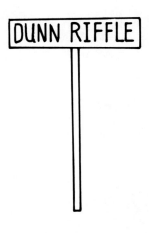

By Michael L. Walker

DIAGRAM 1 - DUNN RIFFLE (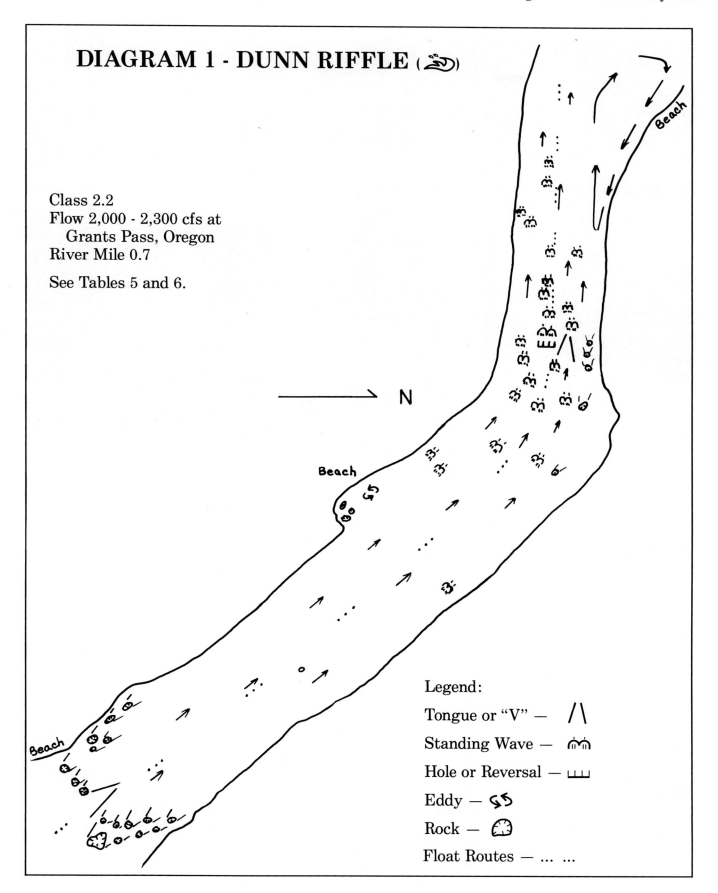)

Class 2.2
Flow 2,000 - 2,300 cfs at
    Grants Pass, Oregon
River Mile 0.7

See Tables 5 and 6.

N

Beach

Beach

Beach

Legend:

Tongue or "V" — /\

Standing Wave — ⌒⌒

Hole or Reversal — ⊔⊔

Eddy — ꙅꙅ

Rock — ⬭

Float Routes — ... ...

Inflatable Kayakers in Dunn Riffle, River Mile 1.0

Do you have your life vest on? A man in an inflatable (K-79 Tahiti) with a life vest in his Tahiti (but not on) died floating Dunn in 1983. He was on the bottom of the Rogue downriver of Dunn for three days. In the interest of fun, I am not going to identify any more of these events in this river log. However, there are more individuals who did not wear a vest with tragic results (see Table 8).

A safety tip for all riffles is to be aware of the others in your craft in relationship to your paddle, especially in a ducky. In many cases your worst injury or banging will be a knock on the head from a neighbor's paddle during high white water moments. Another courtesy is to be aware of the float needs of other craft around you. Don't get someone else in trouble because you were too close to them which now finds them maneuvering to keep you out of trouble.

Sloppy Nostalgia (🙂)

The early days found us bodysurfing (by accident) the reversal and standing wave in Dunn with inner-tubes. We were batting about 500 in that we made it through the reversal with our inner-tubes in about half the attempts.

The first time as a captain of an inflatable K-79 yellow Tahiti I was reluctant yet excited. The run was from Hog Creek to Indian Mary Park. My friend Clay Dickerson talked me into going. He had two K-79's. I would take his daughter, Karren, and he would take his son, Eric.

Everything was fine until we started running Dunn. The damn thing would not go where I directed it. I don't know what Karren thought prior to put-in at Hog Creek, but I was trying to pull off the adult male bluff: I would macho it and pretend I knew what I was doing. It

By Michael L. Walker

didn't work. At the Dunn reversal I was going for it, and the right tube went high. I climbed cat-like to the high side and presto, Karren and I were in the drink. Karren has not gone floating with me since. Sorry, Karren. Obviously I didn't know something about inflatables.

Trampolining Dunn is another interesting story. We found my brothers Jon and Dale in the reversal. Jon, a left-handed, hairy, bearded "friendly" man called Bear, at 6'3" and 285 pounds, was in the bow of a ducky while Dale, a left-handed, laid-back, bearded dude (Fuzz) at 5'10" and a modest 175 pounds was in the stern. The bow of the ducky went into the hole of the reversal first with the Fuzz in the stern and four feet higher than the Bear. OK so far, but as the ducky's bow crashed through and over the reversal the Bear was lifted up and up, while the stern and Fuzz moved to the bottom of the hole. Panic city! In Fuzz's mind it appeared that the Bear was going to lose it and have all of his pounds go tumbling back into the stern and onto Fuzz's modest bod. Up went both of Fuzz's hands (paddle in left one) to protect himself. Now the ducky went over the crest of the reversal with the bow crashing down, resulting in a trampoline effect on the lighter stern section. The Fuzz, not holding on to the raft, went airborne in an arc that landed him outside the ducky. Smile...MAN OVERBOARD!

Another excursion finds the Bear and me, each in an inflatable K-79 Tahiti, running the standing wave and reversal in Dunn a few years ago when the river was strange and playful. I was in the lead and made a perfect drop into the reversal in front of the standing wave, except instead of a fast crush through the wave, my inflatable and I were suddenly perpendicular to the river and still floating in the hole in front of the standing wave. My bow was pointed straight toward the left bank and I was going nowhere. I was looking at this unusual view, when I became startled as I remembered the Bear had been about five seconds behind me. He was coming straight at me! My immediate future was flip-city time!

His inflatable hit mine hard and I was softly (I don't know why) pushed out into the flow of the riffle once again. Now my brother was stuck in the same position I had previously found myself. He stayed a few seconds and was also spit out as softly as I had been. We discussed this adventure and were so excited that we decided to float the riffle again. We packed our inflatables on our backs and headed upriver on the right bank. Never again--there was no trail. We hopped from rock to rock, got scratched by blackberry bushes, fought willows, wandered through shallow water, and became hot and sweaty. I was looking for snakes but didn't see any. Our second run through Dunn was exciting, but normal. Well...maybe next year.

History (■)

Dunn Riffle was named for a man who drowned here in the early days. In those days there were also rocks and boulders in most of the major riffles. Glen Wooldridge, an early, famous, drift-boater, cleared Dunn Riffle in 1949 as well as most of the other major riffles on this stretch of the river by blasting the rocks with powder (i.e., Ennis, Galice Chute, Galice Store, Rocky, Mine, and Wooldridge riffles) (Arman 1982).

By Michael L. Walker

Inflatable Kayaker in Hellgate Riffle Hole, River Mile 1.2

1.2 RIVER MILE, HELLGATE RIFFLE

Riffle Class and Length (🛶)

The Hellgate Riffle (#3) is a Class I (1.3) if the floater hits the hole (right bank) in the first part of this white water section. The drift distance is approximately 300 yards.

How To (💡)

There are two distinct white water sections comprising the Hellgate Riffle. The start of the riffle is right of midriver down center of the "V" slick past rocks in midriver on the left. Left river has sandpaper or small choppy waves over shallows. There is a great inflatable hole on the extreme right at the first white water section halfway through the riffle. This is a must for white water mania inflatable nuts as the hole is bouncy! The second white water stretch follows quickly. You should approach midriver at "V" for standing waves.

Left of "V" is another hole or rocks depending on river flow. Don't smack the house-sized rock on the left bank at the end of the run, especially if you are thin-skinned (see Diagram 2).

1.4 RIVER MILE, BRIDGE RIFFLE

Riffle Class and Length (🛶)

Bridge Riffle (#4) is a Class I (0.5) riffle with a drift distance of approximately 200 yards.

How To (💡)

This easy riffle starts under the Hellgate Bridge. You should maintain a midriver position. Inflatable kayakers can run near left bank for a small hole, but watch out after the hole at low-river flows for a sleeper. After the sleeper the flow of this "V" at midriver pushes to the right bank at end of float.

By Michael L. Walker

DIAGRAM 2 - HELLGATE RIFFLE (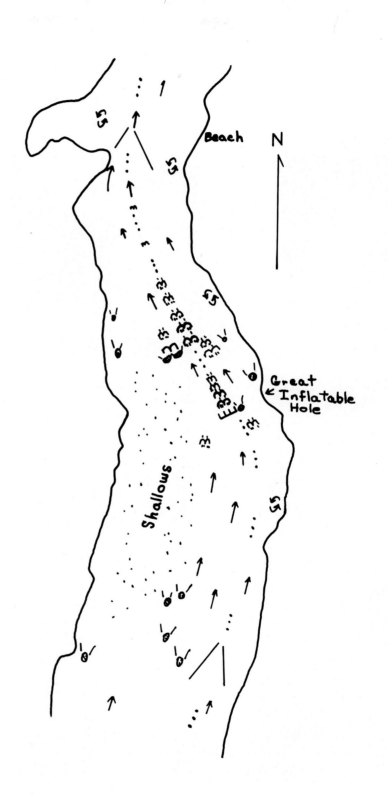)

Class 1.3
Flow c,000 - 2,300 cfs
    at Grants Pass, Oregon
River Mile 1.2

See Tables 5 and 6.

Legend:

Tongue or "V" — /\

Standing Wave — ⌒⌒⌒

Hole or Reversal — ⊔⊔

Eddy — ᎦᏚ

Rock — ⬭

Float Routes — ... ...

Evening "Feeling" While Looking Toward Hellgate Riffle, River Mile 1.3

By Michael L. Walker

Hellgate Bridge, River Mile 1.4

The bridge is higher than the level of the highest officially recorded flood of 1964.

1.4 RIVER MILE, HELLGATE BRIDGE

Built after the 1964 flood, this bridge is a modern steel bridge which replaced the second earlier Hellgate Bridge. At 70 feet above normal summer flow, it is at a new site about 1,000 feet upriver of the old bridge site. Green willows surround the supports of the bridge. The water is too shallow for jumping off the new bridge. Don't even think about jumping unless your goal in life is to acquire a pair of shorter legs! There is a dirt road which provides access to the river on right bank (trail on left bank).

1.7 RIVER MILE, STRATTON CREEK RECREATION SITE

Description (▼)

Major masses of serpentine rock on the right bank upmountain clue you that you are just upriver of the Stratton Creek Recreation Site, a day-use area, managed by the Bureau of Land Management (BLM). Sensitive or rare plants are usually associated with serpentine rock. The recreation site has the best accessible sandy beach on this stretch of the river. The drift past the site is leisurely with slow water. Road access is on both banks. There are toilets, waste cans, and parking areas provided. There is two-tenths of a mile of flat water after leaving the beach at the recreation site before arriving at Indian Mary Park Boat Landing.

Sloppy Nostalgia (😊)

If you have time, build a small sand castle at the Stratton Creek Recreation Site, or come back another day and build a large one. I have spent many casual hours here claiming large amounts of sandy beach for my castle constructions.

During the evenings I have seen a family of otters playing in the shallows on the west bank. Look for otter trails in the sandy banks where they scamper up and down slippery mud-covered slopes, sliding into the water on their stomachs. The river otter is a three to five foot long, slender, sleek-bodied, aquatic weasel with a thick, blunt, heavily-furred tail. Perhaps the best swimmers of all American mammals, otters can remain underwater for up to four minutes. Otter dams here are probably carefully concealed burrows dug into a bank on the river's edge, and the entrance is probably underwater.

"I like the feeling of the rays of hot sun beating down on my drenched skin after a water fight and just laying back as the craft carries me slowly downriver. You can almost imagine yourself floating in mid-air--all your worries behind and the skin on your face half wet, half dry, with your cheeks beginning to burn."

Karen Walker, Summer of 1988

Sandcastle at Stratton Creek Recreation Site: Rooms $35 per Night, River Mile 1.5

By Michael L. Walker

Another year finds four of us in a ducky on our way past the Stratton Creek Recreation Site to Indian Mary Park for a celebration and reunion of teachers and students of the now-closed Hugo Elementary School. The ducky was already wounded with a two-foot tear in the bottom from a rock in the Hellgate Riffle. Becky Halstead and I were in the stern looking at the bottom of the raft which was full of water. The Bear and another friend, Cynthia, were in the bow. Suddenly a water fight broke out between Cynthia and the Bear resulting in a playful wrestling match that lead to both of them falling to the bottom of the ducky mixed up with paddles, water buckets, a dry bag, and water. Becky and I found this amusing. The situation became hilarious as the Bear and Cynthia disappeared through the bottom of the ducky and into the river as the two-foot tear exploded into a 10-foot hole. Becky and I began laughing so hard we almost fell off the ducky, which was at that point a huge inner-tube as the raft was completely bottomless. All right, more patch material!

History (■)

The first Hellgate Bridge was built in 1913 at a site between the sandy beaches on the recreation site and the Indian Mary Park boat landing. It was destroyed in 1927 by a flood and later rebuilt slightly upriver of the sandy beaches. I can remember seeing the flood waters of 1964 rushing over the running boards of the second Hellgate Bridge. You can still see the eastern earthy foundation of the second bridge.

I also remember as a teenager listening to Buck, an old man who lived up Buckhorn Mountain from the bridge. One time my troop of boy scouts hiked up the mountain to his home. He showed us his tree house he lived in and large holes he and others had dug looking for gold which he believed had been buried by white men escaping a pursuing band of Indians. He even said he had found a little of the gold!

Buck could always be recognized by his long, full, white beard and hat. Buck also talked about some of the large rocks by the bridge and the special names by which the Indians used to recognize them. Unfortunately, I forgot the names.

By Michael L. Walker

Dale and Karen Walker at Stratton Creek Recreation Site, River Mile 1.5

By Michael L. Walker

Inflatable Kayaker in Hellgate Riffle Hole, River Mile 1.2

Ducky Rafters in Hellgate Riffle Hole, River Mile 1.2

By Michael L. Walker

INDIAN MARY PARK BOAT LANDING TO ENNIS RIFFLE BOAT LANDING

Refer to the map entitled "Indian Mary Park Boat Landing to Ennis Riffle Boat Landing" for a geographic description of the major points of float interest (see Map 5). This river stretch has a white water difficulty rating of WW 0.2, the least difficult of all the stretches on the Hog Run (see Appendix B).

2.5 RIVER MILE, INDIAN MARY PARK BOAT LANDING

Indian Mary Park Boat Landing Description (●)

There is a paved road to a concrete boat launch area and parking for approximately 20 vehicles on-site. There is also a large parking area just up the hill about 50 yards. People fishing will usually be found on a rocky point just below the boat landing on the left bank.

Facilities (▲)

Indian Mary Park is run by Josephine County and is the best large daytime recreation area and camping area in the county, probably in southern Oregon. It has everything (see Table 9). I mean it. Try it, I have, and I love it!

Drift Distance (←→)/Time (🕐) To Ennis Riffle Boat Landing - 2.2 miles/1 to 1 1/4 hours

History (■)

A sign at the entrance of Indian Mary Park reads, "Historic Indian Mary Park, Smallest Indian Reservation ever created, granted to Indian Mary by U.S. Government in 1885 in recognition of gratitude to her father, Umpqua Joe, who gave the alarm which saved white settlers in this area from a planned massacre" (see section on History, Indian Wars; and

Grants Pass Courier 1935). The site of Umpqua Joe and Indian Mary's house was close to where the caretaker's residence is today. The Indian Mary Park boat ramp is the location where Joe operated a ferry (USSGO 1856). Go down to the boat ramp and gaze across the Rogue a little upriver. It is not obvious, but if you know you are looking for a ferry landing, you will see the old road. The ferry landing has been washed away long ago. Go across to the other side of the river and walk the old road, a raised level area. You will discover old rock culverts in the old road bed.

The old road bed has a trail on it starting as a fishermen's path at the north end of the Stratton Creek Recreation Site and paralleling the river on the north bank to across the river from the boat ramp where the old road ends. The fishermen's trail continues to Taylor Creek Gorge. The size and shape of the trail between No Name Gulch II and Stratton Creek reminds one of what a mule trail must have looked like in the late 1800's.

Mary was later married and became Mary Peco. She became a widow when her husband and her father killed each other in a gun fight (Booth 1975). "Umpqua Joe, his son-in-law, and other members of the family were buried on the north side of the river near the ferry landing. In later years, Massie, who took over the ferry business, uncovered some of their remains while excavating for a house site" (Siskiyou National Forest). Massie was an early pioneer. Later Mary married again and became Mary Peters.

There is another wooden sign across the road from the entrance to Indian Mary Park which reads, "Umpqua Joe Trail." The trail is approximately two miles long and of medium difficulty.

Notes (📖)

The river here is a continuation of the slow water which started upriver from the Stratton Creek Recreation Site. There is a small beach in the park on the left bank.

By Michael L. Walker

MAP 5
INDIAN MARY PARK BOAT LANDING
TO ENNIS RIFFLE BOAT LANDING

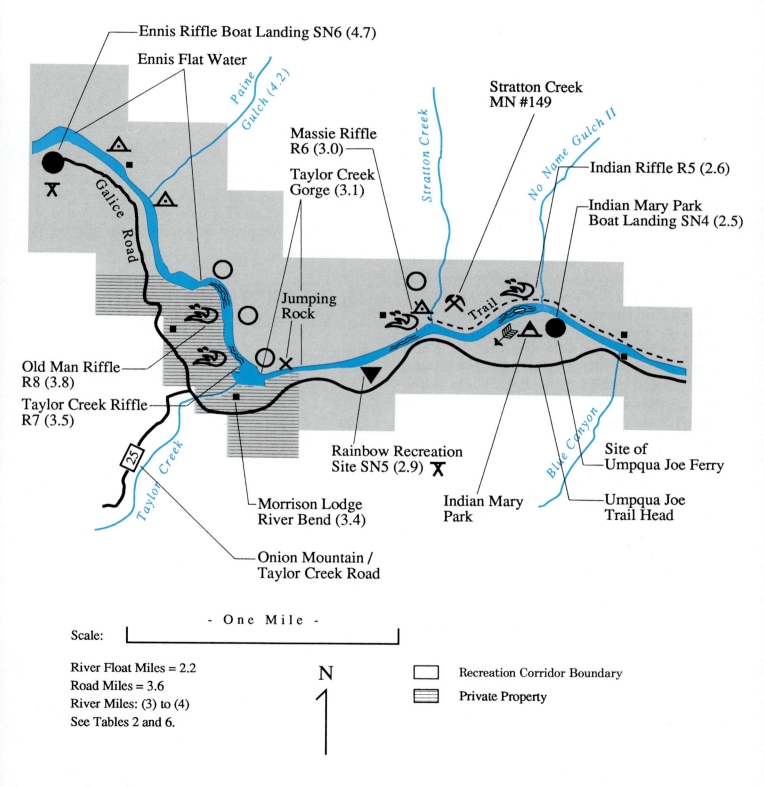

Ennis Riffle Boat Landing SN6 (4.7)

Ennis Flat Water

Paine Gulch (4.2)

Stratton Creek

Stratton Creek MN #149

No Name Gulch II

Massie Riffle R6 (3.0)

Indian Riffle R5 (2.6)

Taylor Creek Gorge (3.1)

Indian Mary Park Boat Landing SN4 (2.5)

Galice Road

Jumping Rock

Trail

Old Man Riffle R8 (3.8)

Taylor Creek Riffle R7 (3.5)

Taylor Creek

Blue Canyon

Rainbow Recreation Site SN5 (2.9)

Site of Umpqua Joe Ferry

25

Morrison Lodge River Bend (3.4)

Indian Mary Park

Umpqua Joe Trail Head

Onion Mountain / Taylor Creek Road

Scale: - One Mile -

River Float Miles = 2.2
Road Miles = 3.6
River Miles: (3) to (4)
See Tables 2 and 6.

N

Recreation Corridor Boundary

Private Property

By Michael L. Walker

2.6 RIVER MILE, INDIAN RIFFLE

Riffle Class and Length (🏊)

Indian Riffle (#5) is a Class I (0.5) riffle with a drift distance of approximately 400 yards.

How To (💡)

There is a small gravel island in the middle of the river shortly downriver from the beach at Indian Mary Park. Guess what I call it...Indian Mary Island. The island creates a riffle with two approaches. The left-of-island approach is a "V" where the main flow sweeps along the left bank. You should maintain midriver on the left approach to avoid debris sometimes sticking out from the shore. This debris could create a strainer. A strainer can be brush, fallen trees, or anything else that allows the current to sweep through, but pins an inflatable or raft and floaters. These are lethal. Thank God there are very few of these situations on this stretch. The second approach is right of the island following the "V" where you maintain midriver position to avoid water flow forcing you into the right bank. Afterwards, the water shallows at the end of the island on the right. You should bear left toward the new "V."

2.9 RIVER MILE, RAINBOW RECREATION SITE (🗙)

This access is left bank and situated on a small, level wooded area immediately upriver of Taylor Creek Gorge and downstream from Indian Mary Park. It is an inviting spot at the bottom of the steep canyon walls. There is a screened parking area for about six vehicles, fire rings, toilets, garbage cans, and picnic tables at this site, which is mostly used by fishermen. There is a short, pristine trail to the river which takes only a few minutes to walk.

There are isolated scenic views of the river at vegetation breaks on the trail and a small beach at the end of the trail by the river. In emergencies it can be used by the floater to leave the river prior to entering the Taylor Creek Gorge.

3.0 RIVER MILE, MASSIE RIFFLE

Riffle Class and Length (🏊)

Massie Riffle (#6) is a Class I (0.5) riffle with a drift distance of approximately 200 yards.

How To (💡)

This is an easy riffle that starts just downriver of Stratton Creek which enters the Rogue on the right bank. You should float the "V" near the left bank to splash through several waves. It is shallow right bank of the "V" or tongue with more sandpaper (small choppy waves over shallows).

Sloppy Nostalgia (😊)

Another story involves my children. You can imagine how nervous a fellow gets the first time he takes his children on a float, no matter how commonplace it might be. My son Neil was six and my daughter Karen was thirteen at the time. Besides, my ex-wife's lawyer had told me that she would have my butt if Neil or

Floater Convoy Just Prior to Taylor Creek Gorge, River Mile 3.1. Massie Riffle in the Background.

By Michael L. Walker

Indian Mary Island is Upriver, River Mile 2.6

Ducky Floaters above Massie Riffle, River Mile 2.9

By Michael L. Walker

Karen went floating white water with me during the summers when they visited. Well, at Fuzz's urging (he was taking his sons, Jeff and Brock), I went along with it. Afterall there was not even a Class I riffle on the stretch from Indian Mary Park to the Ennis Riffle Boat Landing. Fuzz and I were having a beverage and were thoroughly enjoying our little float together with the kids when we hit Massie Riffle (Class 0.5). Neil was crouched down in the ducky so that only his head was looking over the starboard tube. He was dry at the time when a freak wave crashed over the tube into his face. His eyes became huge white saucers and his body instantly wet, a blond drowned rat. We all laughed and nothing was said for a minute until Karen asked whether that was white water. The old man, thinking fast in the water agreed that it was close, but actually only swift water. Do I know how to dance! Smile. Actually, I must admit that I found out that my ex's bark is worse than her bite. Karen told her about the float that evening during a telephone conversation and my ex never said anything until a year later when, in another telephone conversation, she laughingly said, "Swift water, huh?"

History (■)

Massie Riffle takes its name from a man named Massie, who leased the property now known as Indian Mary Park from Indian Mary shortly before 1900. Massie, among other things, owned the ferry at the site which operated until the first Hellgate Bridge was built in 1913 (Hill 1976). It is assumed that the ferry landing site was the one Umpqua Joe used.

It does not exist anymore, but do any of you remember the yellow barn? It and a residence were on a bench north of the river below Stratton Creek. K. L. Olson was the last occupant of the residence which was associated with the Stratton Creek Placer Mine (MN # 149). The historic mine is up Stratton Creek on the right bank. It's mining claim dates from 1893 (USDI 1965).

Notes (📖)

An osprey nest (△) is located on the west side of Stratton Creek up the hill from the river. The osprey, also known as the "fish hawk," has a white head and lots of white below. They mate for life. There is a great place to dry camp above Massie Riffle on the right bank downriver from Stratton Creek (see section on Management Zones). There are lots of free blackberries on the north side of the river at this point. Usually only the birds get them.

3.1 RIVER MILE,
TAYLOR CREEK GORGE

Except for Ennis Riffle you will now pass through approximately three miles of flat water, starting with the spectacular scenery of Taylor Creek Gorge and ending at Carpenter's Island. The gorge sometimes goes by the name of "Windy Gap" (■). Windy Gap was actually where the Galice Road high above the canyon tunneled it's way through a ridge which went all the way to the river (Hill 1976). This stretch is a good place to observe some of the birds which use the river (see Table 10). You can usually see common mergansers here, where in the summer, small troops of young ducks follow their moms all in a line. The daddy duck has a dark green head and a long white body.

The drift distance through the gorge is approximately two-tenths of a mile. The water is flat in the gorge where the tightening cliffs close in on you (approximately 100 feet up to the Galice Road on the left bank). Don't trust friendly smiles from other floaters in this stretch as you are likely to suddenly hear the brief warning of the word "ATTACK" as another water fight is initiated.

Jumpers at Gorge Jumping Rock, River Mile 3.4

Late summer 1987 from one of the two view points above the gorge I saw an armada of drift boats in the Taylor Creek Gorge during a salmon run. Line-over-line was the rule. Boy, were they having fun.

There is an excellent spot to stop in the canyon for diving and jumping from a rock into deep water (✗). At 13 feet tall this is a great starter jumping rock. Gorge Jumping Rock is about half-way into Taylor Creek Gorge and can be identified opposite a relatively recent slide on the left canyon wall.

If you will mentally continue up the canyon wall across from the jumping rock, you will encounter the Galice Road and a gravel overlook. The overlook is a great place to take pictures. It is also the location of a remnant of the historic Galice Road in the form of a concrete retainer wall. Boy, that road used to be close to the edge of the cliff. In the spring you will also find mobs of cliff swallows attending to their gourd-like homes which are attached to the cliff above the road.

By Michael L. Walker

3.4 RIVER MILE, MORRISON LODGE RIVER BEND/TAYLOR CREEK

The main flow of the river bends right, but there is a large area of flat water forward and left in this large river bend. It is private property on the left bank from the river bend to after Old Man Riffle. Morrison Lodge (■), a long time private resort on the shore of the bend, was established by L. Lloyd Morrison in 1944, the year I was born (Hill 1976).

Taylor Creek enters the Rogue at this river bend. The lower portion of Taylor Creek Valley is beautiful with trees, rock outcrops, cliffs, and scenic views from the Taylor Creek/Onion Mountain Road which is a winding one and one-half lane paved road. Approximately six miles up the valley on the Taylor Creek Road from the Galice Road junction is a small but beautiful swimming hole near the road on Siskiyou National Forest land. The water is cold and clear even in the hottest summer. There are jumping and diving rocks. You can have a fun lunch or evening hot dog roast here.

Taylor Creek Road connects with the Onion Mountain Road and Hayes Hill on U.S. Highway 199. This 33-mile drive offers great vistas of the Grants Pass and Illinois valleys. Thirteen miles along the way the Big Pine Campground boasts the world's second largest ponderosa pine, while Serpentine Lookout and Onion Mountain Lookout offer interesting side trips (Josephine County 1981).

3.5 RIVER MILE, TAYLOR CREEK RIFFLE

Riffle Class and Length ( )

Taylor Creek Riffle (#7) is a Class I (0.7) riffle with a drift distance of approximately 200 yards.

How To ( )

This approach has a large, low rock formation on the left bank. Your approach should be made toward a small gravel bar on the right side of the river. You may pass left or right of the gravel bar. Maintain midposition after passing the gravel bar as water sweeps to right bank where the river narrows. There is a strong shear zone and hydraulics after passing right bank where water flows join from several directions.

Sloppy Nostalgia (☺)

I have flipped in inflatables twice in this riffle as a result of complacency and the shear zone. One of those times I was trying to impress my date. Poor show.

History (■)

Taylor Creek was named for Mary Taylor Crow's family who were early pioneers. They lived at the mouth of Taylor Creek (Hill 1976).

Notes ( )

There is a solitary osprey nest (○) high on the ridge, right bank from the riffle. You can see it from the Galice Road.

3.8 RIVER MILE, OLD MAN RIFFLE

Riffle Class and Length (🚣)

Old Man Riffle (#8) is a Class 0.5 riffle with a drift distance of approximately 300 yards.

How To (💡)

This is an easy riffle, just float midriver. There is a small wave at the bottom of this riffle.

Sloppy Nostalgia (☺)

I visited home one year when I was a pilot in the Navy and I wanted to float. My idea was met with some resistance as it was April and cool, but it was a sunny day and finally I talked the Fuzz, Bear, and another friend, Clay Dickerson, into making a run. Wrong...it showered, we got soaked and miserable. It became so cold (see Table 11 and Graph 2) our knees clattered . We stopped at the bar below Old Man Riffle to whizz and there we had a few problems. Our hands were numb and we had difficulty getting our jeans unzipped, and when we finally did, we couldn't find our peters. They were hiding out somewhere. It's tough to whizz when you have a very tiny whizzer, and it's also painful. Another lesson was learned. This time the lesson was about the dangers of initial hypothermia, a dangerous situation. Now I have a farmer-john which is a wet suit that looks like coveralls. After that was over, the beautiful end of a wet day was a rainbow in the bright wet mist bending toward the bar across the river.

Notes (📖)

There are osprey nests (○) high on the right bank at the top of the dead snags near the bottom of Old Man Riffle. As you know, osprey mate for life. You may not know that after wintering in Mexico, they return in the early spring and nest near water where they feed on fish.

Most osprey live about 15 years and come back year after year to the same nest site. One of the sites at Old Man Riffle has been very productive as I have seen young in the nest between July and August for many years. There is also a great blue heron rookery (△) in this area.

3.9 RIVER MILE, ENNIS FLAT WATER

This is a long, wide, slow, stretch of flat water approximately seven-tenths of a mile in length. The drift time to Ennis Riffle from here is approximately 40 minutes.

Notes (📖)

The long reaches of the quiet calms of this stretch of flat water can get you if you're hyper, or they can be wonderfully, leisurely holistic (what the hell does that mean?). It feels like forever until Ennis Riffle. I'm hyper... smile. In emergencies, the Galice Road is very close to the left bank. It's a great place for more water-fight action.

Paine Gulch is on the right bank about one-half way through the Ennis Flat Water stretch. The mouth of the gulch has a small beach which is loaded with round, smooth, flat rocks perfect for skipping over the river water. My son, Neil (11 years) and I have spent many happy lunch hours here. Ah, those days...

"Keep not the white water from its pleasure seekers".

Mikie Walker, 1985.

Dry, Hot, Summer-view of the Osprey Nest above Old Man Riffle, River Mile 3.8

By Michael L. Walker

ENNIS RIFFLE BOAT LANDING TO GALICE STORE BOAT LANDING

Refer to the map entitled "Ennis Riffle Boat Landing to Galice Store Boat Landing" for a geographic description of the major points of float interest (see Map 6). This river stretch has a white water index of WW 0.7, the most difficult on the Hog Run (see Appendix B).

4.7 RIVER MILE, ENNIS RIFFLE BOAT LANDING

Ennis Boat Landing Description (●)

There is a narrow paved road to a concrete boat launch area and a gravel parking area for approximately 20 to 25 vehicles near the boat launch area. There is endless parking space on the bar away from the boat landing.

Facilities (✗)

The Ennis Bar is huge (approximately 2,300 feet long). Facilities of the day-use area include toilets and garbage cans as well as the boat launch area which is at the east end or top of the bar. A river bar is an accumulation of sand, gravel, or rock in the river channel or along the bank.

Drift Distance (↔) /Time (🕐) To Galice Store Boat Landing - 2.1 Miles/ 3/4 to 1 hour

Sloppy Nostalgia (☺)

Fuzz and I and his sons, Jeff (13 years) and Brock (10 years), and my son, Neil (9 years), had another great camping and rafting trip based out of Ennis Bar. The lower end of the bar is quite sandy near the river and great for camping and sandcastle building. What I especially remember about this trip was Brock's and Neil's adventure at water fighting. They each had a small inner-tube and a gallon milk bucket with the end cut off, the ultimate arsenal for the sneak attack. They would float in the eddy across the river which was visually screened by some low rocks and grasses. Floaters of Ennis Riffle who went along the right bank would travel slowly by the eddy and then discover the two smiling children. Smiling is the clue. Neil and Brock were wearing their water buckets as hats and looked fairly harmless as they let the floaters go by. At this time a few of the larger males would become suspicious and in large commanding voices indicate what the two children should not do...to no avail. The two children let out exuberant whoops and, splash, splash, here we go again, the sneak water attack. I loved it!

Notes (📖)

Ennis Bar seems to be a place where you can always find an angler. The Rogue is well known for its half-pounder, or late summer/early fall steelhead. These two to five pound fish return to the Rogue after an average of three months of ocean life. The winter steelhead return to the Rogue from mid-November to March. The winter steelhead usually weigh between 5 to 15 pounds with an occasional whopper topping 20 pounds.

4.8 RIVER MILE, ENNIS RIFFLE (🏊)

Ennis Riffle (#9) is a Class I (1.4) riffle with a drift distance of approximately 600 yards. At a higher water level (around 3,500 cfs measured at Lost Creek Dam) Ennis Riffle is a Class II+ to a III− rapid. Ennis Riffle to Grave Creek avoids the first 4.7 miles of river and eliminates between 2 and 2 1/2 hours of float time, making it an excellent place for late-starters.

By Michael L. Walker

MAP 6
ENNIS RIFFLE BOAT LANDING TO
GALICE STORE BOAT LANDING

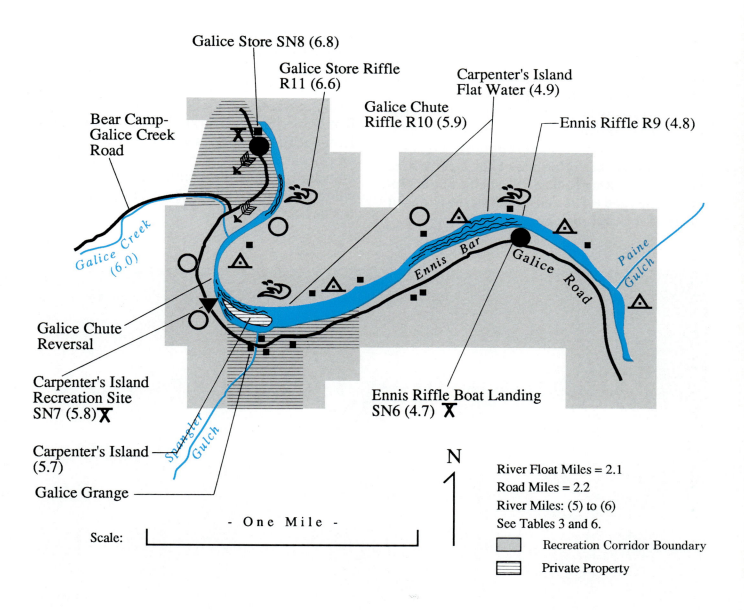

Galice Store SN8 (6.8)

Galice Store Riffle
R11 (6.6)

Carpenter's Island
Flat Water (4.9)

Galice Chute
Riffle R10 (5.9)

Ennis Riffle R9 (4.8)

Bear Camp-
Galice Creek
Road

Galice Creek
(6.0)

Galice Chute
Reversal

Carpenter's Island
Recreation Site
SN7 (5.8)

Carpenter's Island
(5.7)

Galice Grange

Spangler Gulch

Ennis Bar

Galice Road

Paine Gulch

Ennis Riffle Boat Landing
SN6 (4.7)

N

River Float Miles = 2.1
Road Miles = 2.2
River Miles: (5) to (6)
See Tables 3 and 6.

Recreation Corridor Boundary

Private Property

- One Mile -

Scale:

How To (💡)

The route is to maintain the "V" slick close to left bank and avoid shallows at the top and rocks at the bottom of the run on the right. There are many large rocks in the middle of the river, both above the water and submerged. An alternate approach for inflatable kayakers is the run on the right side of the river where you follow another broken "V" slick while scraping submerged rocks and avoiding the exposed rocks of a small rock garden.

Sloppy Nostalgia (🙂)

On another one-day float trip several years ago, a group of us were in two rubber duckies and the water level was high. It was a fairly typical float trip until we found ourselves in Ennis Riffle which at that water level was an exciting Class III rapid. Fuzz was the nincompoop navigator with his head in the clouds because his ducky hit a huge sleeper just barely level with the surface of the river (quite a hole on the downriver side). He was at the stern of the ducky when it smacked the sleeper. At the sound of the smack he flew through the air past his girl friend (now we know what he was doing) and our niece, Marci, a dedicated novice floater. The raft was stopped and the two women were stuck fast with their raft firmly wrapped on the sleeper in the middle of Ennis Riffle. Who says you cannot wrap a raft on the bathtub run? It stayed there for about 30 minutes until we could pull it off. Guess what the women talked about for the next two weeks? Smile.

Happy Ducky Floaters in Ennis Riffle, River Mile 4.9

By Michael L. Walker

4.9 RIVER MILE, CARPENTER'S ISLAND FLAT WATER

Carpenter's Island flat water starts half-way down along Ennis bar after the riffle. The drift distance to Carpenter's Island is approximately eight-tenths of a mile. It is time again to consider white water combat. Find your bailer and look for dry floaters.

Notes (📖)

There is an osprey's nest (◯) right bank about halfway through this stretch of flat water. The bulky stick nest is high on top of a dead Douglas fir snag. They only eat fish which they swoop down on from a hover position 50 to 150 feet above the river. It's a great sight when the bird attacks with a sudden plunge from the hover to hitting the water, sometimes going completely under trying to snag the fish with its claws.

Osprey nests can be lined with strange objects:

"Objects found in osprey's nests include shorts, bath towels, garden rake, rope, broom, barrel staves, hoops, fishnet, toy boat, old shoes, fish lines, straw hat, rag doll, bottles, tin cans, shells, and sponges" (Harrison 1979).

This section of the river marks the half-way spot for the Memorial Day hydroplane jet boat races which start at the Riverside Park in Grants Pass. The jet boats turn-around here above Carpenter's Island to finish the last half of the race back to the city park.

5.7 RIVER MILE, CARPENTER'S ISLAND

Carpenter's Island is a large island in the middle of the Rogue. The drift distance past the island is approximately 150 yards.

Guess why the island is named Carpenter's Island? You'll never guess. Maybe? Yeah, that's right, a man named Carpenter used to have a store near the island (Hill 1976).

5.7 RIVER MILE, GALICE CHUTE RIFFLE

Riffle Class and Length (🏊)

Galice Chute Riffle (#10) is a Class II (2.0) riffle if the floater hits the reversal. The drift distance is approximately 600 yards.

How To (💡)

In flows of 1,800 cfs or more you will miss the rocks in the Galice Chute Riffle. The water level at this flow is deep enough that you do not scrape the bottom of your craft too badly.

The riffle starts at the upriver side of Carpenter's Island. Approach the right side of the island down "V" slick close to the island. The river definitely starts to move at this point. The "V" disappears into sandpaper right bank. Pay attention as minor maneuvering is necessary around several small submerged rocks along the island. The float may also be run to the left of the island.

As you pass the end of Carpenter's Island the river converges as the river water merges from both sides of the island. You are approximately halfway through the riffle with about 300 yards to run. You should now bear left of a low ridge of rocks on the right while acknowledging the weak shear zone where the river converges. The approach to the major white water of the chute begins now at a point through the "V." Watch out for a rock or hole midriver (depending on river flow).

There are two approaches at this point depending on the floater's goals: 1. You can go right of midriver into large standing waves, or 2. You can go left of midriver, which leads you into the major reversal and the wildest part of this riffle. There is a major standing wave at the start of both approaches. The floater too far left at this point will be pushed into left bank where the river narrows dramatically. Left of midriver is an excellent reversal perpendicular to the river for inflatable kayakers, and there are good standing waves to the right of midriver. Inflatables: be prepared to Brace! Brace! Brace! Floaters can catch the eddies left or right bank for stopping and viewing other floaters running the reversal. This is one of your best white water adventures on this stretch (see Diagram 3).

Sloppy Nostalgia (☺)

August 28, 1988 found "Road Runner" Ed moonlight floating the chute. Ed has a large orange flag with a road runner on it attached to the back of his raft. He is another "friendly." Say hi! The thrill of floating in the moonlight is exciting as your vision is slightly impaired, but your hearing is seemingly enhanced. I have floated in the dark by accident (misjudged the float time) several times. It's sort of scary.

Notes (📖)

It is hard to see from the river as you are concentrating on the riffle, but there are several osprey nests (◯) near the Galice Road across from the Galice chute reversal.

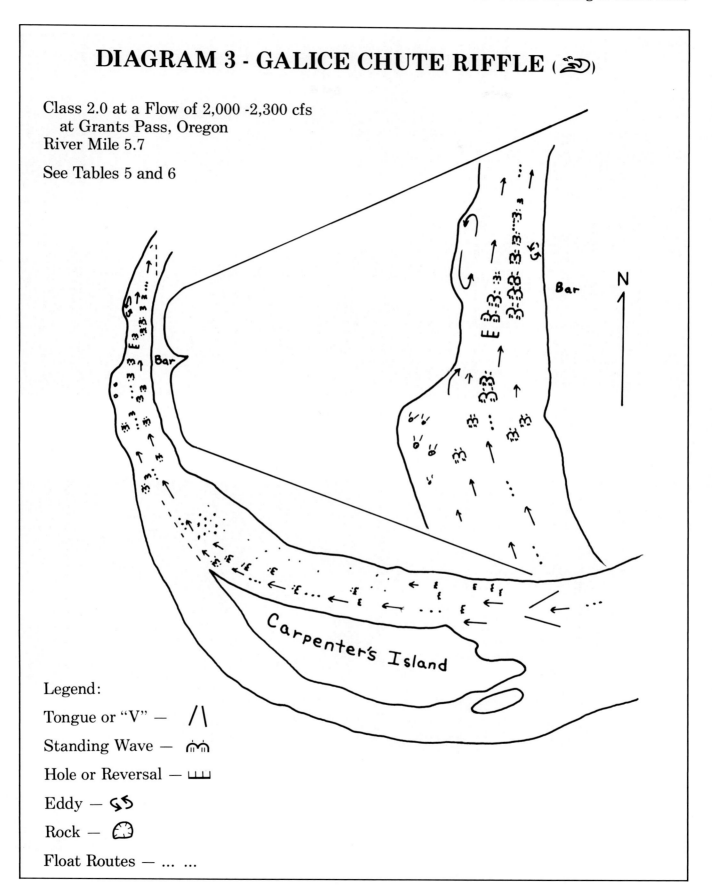

DIAGRAM 3 - GALICE CHUTE RIFFLE

Class 2.0 at a Flow of 2,000 -2,300 cfs
   at Grants Pass, Oregon
River Mile 5.7

See Tables 5 and 6

N

Bar

Bar

Carpenter's Island

Legend:

Tongue or "V" — /\

Standing Wave — ᴍ

Hole or Reversal — ⊔⊔

Eddy — ⧢

Rock — ⬭

Float Routes — ... ...

Inflatable Kayaker in Galice Chute Riffle Hole, River Mile 5.9

Thrill Seeking Ducky Floaters in Galice Chute Riffle, River Mile 5.9

By Michael L. Walker

5.8 RIVER MILE, CARPENTER'S ISLAND RECREATION SITE (▼ ; 🍴)

This beautiful site is a small level area directly below the Galice Road. There is a short trail with good access to the river from a small day-use picnic area which has parking for approximately six cars. There are no toilets. Use is primarily by fishermen in the summer and fall, but it is being used more and more by inflatable kayakers following the scent of a one-half day float to Grave Creek during the summer.

Remember Walter Reese? (■) He died in 1964, but he lived out his lifetime in a full-time residence at the location of today's recreation site (USDI 1965). The residence is gone, but when we visit the area, we can appreciate the beauty he must have seen.

At the mouth of Spangler Gulch is the Galice Grange building which is upriver of the recreation site on the Galice Road. A rustic sign on the building reads, "Western Mining Council, Inc., Lower Grave Creek Chapter Meets Here 3 Sundays each month, 7 p. m., All Welcome." The building was erected as a general store in the 1800's. The building acts as a community center today.

6.0 RIVER MILE, HISTORIC GALICE CREEK

History (⛏ ; 🪶)

There is a sign by the road at Galice Creek which states, "Historic Galice Creek, Old Mining Camp and Scene of Battle of Rogue River and Indian War of 1855 & 1856, Gold Discovered in 1851."

Historic Galice Creek takes its name from Louis Galice, a miner who worked the creek in the early 1850's. Galice Creek was important for its gold and was one of the earliest diggings in Josephine County. A large amount of manual labor and hydraulic mining occurred on Galice Creek.

The lower several miles of the canyon of Galice Creek are still filled with gold mine tailings from hydraulic mining.

Gold mining ultimately resulted in two mining communities developing here, Galiceburg and Skull Bar. Galiceburg was just below Galice Creek. The place now called Galice is close to the site of the other mining community, Skull

Bar. Skull Bar is the name of the gravel bar downriver from the mouth of Galice Creek on the Rogue River. Many human skulls were discovered here in the gravel bar during mining operations. Presumably the area was an Indian burial ground scattered by flood waters (Booth 1975). An Indian battle took place at Skull Bar.

The Chinese were numerous and active in this area during the heyday of mining. I usually think of them when I see small boulders neatly stacked along a creek.

The next historic milestone is the old brown home of Pat and Zora Gallagher's in which they've lived since 1932. It is nestled between Galice Creek and the Galice Road. It was built in the late 1850's as a cook house for gold miners on Galice Creek. After the mining days and prior to 1932, it had been Spee's Resort and was the main house of a seven-cabin camping and fishing place (Atwood 1984).

Notes (📖)

The rusty red soil on a cut-bank of the Galice Road contrasts violently with the riparian greens and mountain oaks, madrones, and firs of the lower valley. You can still see recreational miners today working the lower part of Galice Creek with small dredges. They are friendly; wave to them as you float by.

Want to go to the Oregon coast? It's just 66 miles over the hill from Galice Creek on the scenic Bear Camp Road through Agness and on to the coastal town of Gold Beach.

By Michael L. Walker

Ducky Rafters in Galice Chute Riffle Hole, River Mile 5.9

Spring Time Ducky Floaters Below Galice Chute Riffle, River Mile 6.0

By Michael L. Walker

6.6 RIVER MILE, GALICE STORE RIFFLE

Riffle Class and Length (🏊)

The Galice Store Riffle (#11) is a Class II (2.0) run if the floater goes head-on into the major hole. The drift distance is approximately 300 yards.

How To (💡)

This riffle starts at a small "V" right of midriver. Watch for rocks on the left. The water speed picks up as the river narrows prior to the start of the main section of white water in the Galice Store Riffle, approximately 100 yards past the tongue.

There are two general approaches to the major white water: 1. The least difficult is to miss the hole by sneaking left, and 2. the head-on crash-and-burn approach to the center hole which visibly attracts you to the wildest ride.

For the first approach you stay midriver and then bear left of the large reversal in the middle of the river. Bear right after this wave for a ride through standing waves. Watch for rocks here at lower water levels. The second approach is for the adventuresome straight through the strong standing wave and reversal. Inflatables: be prepared to Brace! Brace! Brace! Depending on the flow, there may be another strong collapsing wave immediately following the reversal. Catch the eddy left bank to reorganize, or hike to float again. There is clear walking access on the left bank from the top of the riffle to the bottom. This is another great riffle and it can be run again and again by carrying your inflatable along the left bank (see Diagram 4).

Inflatable Kayakers at End of Run Through Galice Store Riffle, River Mile 6.7

By Michael L. Walker

DIAGRAM 4 - GALICE STORE RIFFLE (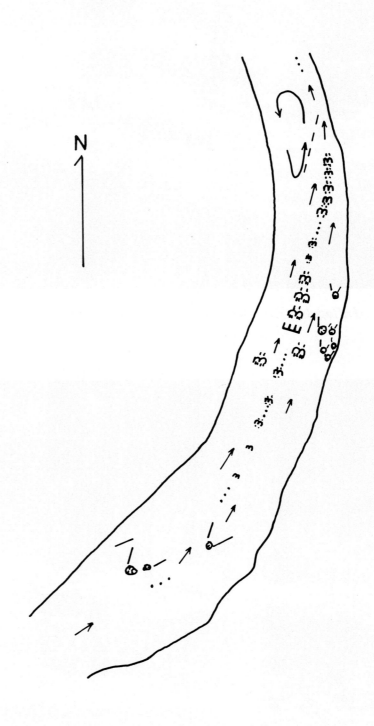)

Class 2.0
Flow 2,000 - 2,300 cfs at
    Grants Pass, Oregon
River Mile 6.6

See Tables 5 and 6

N

Legend:

Tongue or "V" — /\

Standing Waves — ᴍᴍ

Hole or Reversal — ⊔⊔

Eddy — ↺↻

Rock — ⌓

Float Routes — ... ...

By Michael L. Walker

Inflatable Kayaker Break-dancers in Galice Store Riffle Hole, River Mile 6.7

K-79 Inflatable Kayakers Making it Look Easy in Galice Store Riffle Hole, River Mile 6.7

By Michael L. Walker

Sloppy Nostalgia (☺)

The rocks below the hole ate us one day at low flow. We were in a ducky (a 12-foot, used, grey raft I got for $100) and overloaded. I know, I know...I should not have had so many floaters in the paddle raft. I recall my daughter, Karen, wondering about whether it would be safe to go floating. Do you remember Karen? Boy, that question got a great laugh from everyone in the ducky at the Hog Creek Boat Landing. Privately I agreed with her, but the Fuzz had forgotten his ducky and I let it slide. Well anyway, we were having a great run, hit the major hole and standing waves and then a little downriver we came onto the sleeper rocks which were a few inches below the water level...Bam! WOW, HOLY SMOKES, AND WOWEEEE!

Three of our party quickly vanished through the hole torn in the bottom of the raft while the rest of our crew, coughing and sputtering, hung onto another converted inner-tube. The good news was that it was pretty funny once we established that everyone was all right (all had life vests on). The bad news was another dead ducky.

Notes (📖)

It is not uncommon to see deer on the right bank across from this reversal. There is an osprey nest (○) right bank up the hill across from the approach to Galice Store Riffle.

Dead Ducky at Galice Store Boat Landing, River Mile 6.8

Patch Material Holders: Mike, Brock, Jeff, Neil, Dale, and Lana

Photography by Karen Walker

By Michael L. Walker

GALICE STORE BOAT LANDING TO ALMEDA PARK BOAT LANDING

Refer to the map entitled "Galice Store Boat Landing to Almeda Park Boat Landing" for a geographic description of the major points of float interest (see Map 7). This river stretch has a white water difficulty index of WW 0.4 (see Appendix B).

6.8 RIVER MILE, GALICE STORE BOAT LANDING

Galice Store Boat Landing Description (●)

The Galice Store Boat Landing area is privately owned. There is a paved road to a concrete boat launch area and parking for approximately 30-50 vehicles off-site above the landing along the side of the Galice Road. Do not park at the boat ramp area except when actually launching or loading your craft.

Facilities (X)

The historic Galice Store (■) built in 1945 is the successor to the Barlow Store which was built in the gold mining days of the 1850's. The Barlow Store was demolished in the 1950's (Atwood 1984). The site of the old Barlow Store is just north of today's store and next to a redwood tree. Can you find the tree?

The Galice Store provides a full range of services while still retaining a little bit of history. There is a restaurant, outdoor patio, bar, store, gas station, and cabins.

During the summer, country blue grass is provided for your evening entertainment on a flowery, outdoor patio. The music is by Jim Lesher or Buck Harms and Larry Baily of the Country Pride (on alternate weekends). Buck's sister, Joni Harms, has three hit singles.

The store also provides a full range of rafting services--from rental equipment and shuttle services to professional guides. A fun place run by nice people. It is closed for a few weeks during the winter.

Historic Galice Store, River Mile 6.8

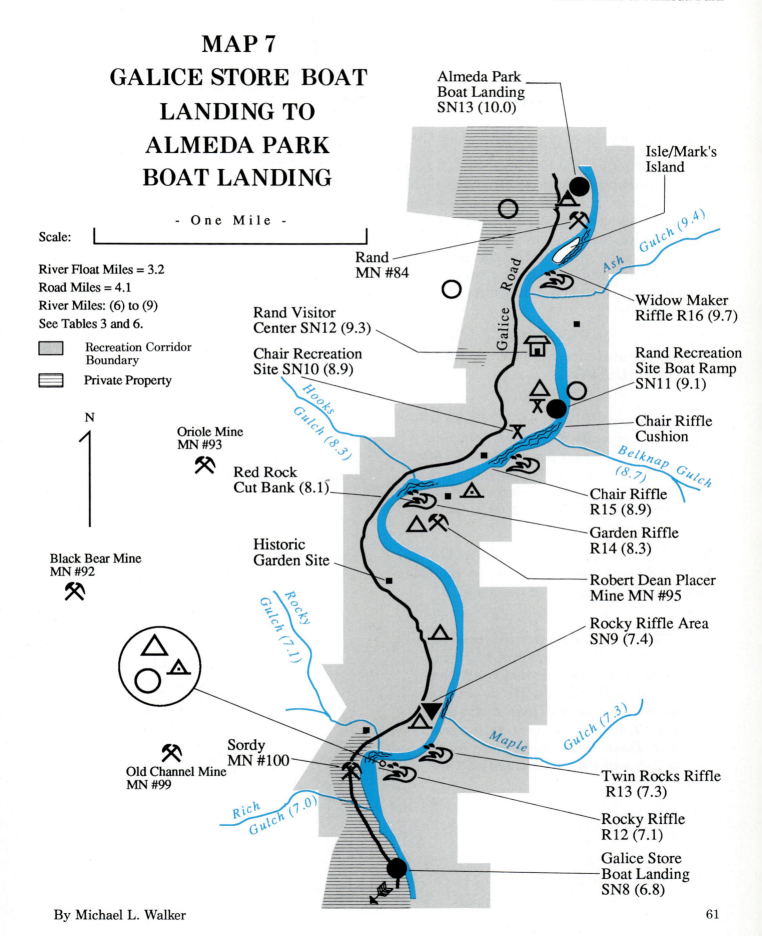

MAP 7
GALICE STORE BOAT LANDING TO ALMEDA PARK BOAT LANDING

- One Mile -

Scale:

River Float Miles = 3.2
Road Miles = 4.1
River Miles: (6) to (9)
See Tables 3 and 6.

Recreation Corridor Boundary

Private Property

N

Oriole Mine MN #93

Red Rock Cut Bank (8.1)

Black Bear Mine MN #92

Historic Garden Site

Hooks Gulch (8.3)

Rocky Gulch (7.1)

Old Channel Mine MN #99

Sordy MN #100

Rich Gulch (7.0)

Almeda Park Boat Landing SN13 (10.0)

Isle/Mark's Island

Rand MN #84

Ash Gulch (9.4)

Widow Maker Riffle R16 (9.7)

Rand Visitor Center SN12 (9.3)

Chair Recreation Site SN10 (8.9)

Galice Road

Rand Recreation Site Boat Ramp SN11 (9.1)

Chair Riffle Cushion

Belknap Gulch (8.7)

Chair Riffle R15 (8.9)

Garden Riffle R14 (8.3)

Robert Dean Placer Mine MN #95

Rocky Riffle Area SN9 (7.4)

Maple Gulch (7.3)

Twin Rocks Riffle R13 (7.3)

Rocky Riffle R12 (7.1)

Galice Store Boat Landing SN8 (6.8)

By Michael L. Walker

Drift Distance (←→) /Time (🕐) To Almeda Park Boat Landing - 3.2 Miles/1 to 1/4 hours

History (⛏; ✎)

The Galice area has had a colorful mining and Indian history.

Rich Gulch enters the Rogue on the left bank a short distance downriver from the Galice Store. Beaver and otter sightings are common on this section of the Rogue. Guess why they called it Rich Gulch? A little less than one mile up the gulch is the site of the Old Channel Mine which in its day was a placer mine known for the large amounts of gold it produced.

The 1857 account book of Ben Adams, the storekeeper at Galice, itemizes some interesting things (USDA):

> *"Flour was 10 cents per lb., bacon 50 cents, overalls $1.50 per pair, and whiskey 25 cents per drink, or $5.00 per quart, rubber boots, for which there appeared to be a large demand from the miners, were $10.00 per pair."*

Today's owners of the Galice Store, Gil (Gilbert) and Mary Lou Thomason, say that some things have changed. For instance:

> *"Flour is 30 cents per lb., bacon is $2.98 per lb., whiskey is $1.50 per drink, and today we don't sell overalls or rubber boots. We do provide memories you will take home with you. Try our famous river burgers. The 'Dunn Riffle' has a class rating of 2.2, and with fries is only $3.00."*

Notes (📖)

The jet boat, "Pepper Lee," is no longer alone on this stretch of the river. A couple of years ago the Pepper Lee was the only commercial jet boat that went downriver of Dunn Riffle. A tremendous increase in jet boat activity since the summers of 1987 and 1988 is a local concern.

Drive cautiously near the store as it is almost always congested with people and vehicles during the summer.

By Michael L. Walker

7.1 RIVER MILE, ROCKY RIFFLE

Riffle Class and Length (🛶)

Rocky Riffle (#12) is a Class I (1.0) riffle with a drift distance of approximately 300 yards.

How To (💡)

There is a good inflatable wave at the top of the riffle left of midriver at higher flows. Later, you should bear right of midriver as the main current wants to sweep you to the left bank as the river bend goes to the right. There are several rocks at the bend that need maneuvering around. You should maintain midriver after the bend into standing waves, the first wave of which is a kick and great for taking pictures of your friends.

History (■)

Rocky Gulch enters the Rogue on the left bank at a point where you are trying to miss the rocks in Rocky Riffle. There are several old mining ditches which start high up Rocky Gulch, swing around the ridge to the east and eventually end up dumping into the Rocky Riffle bar. One ditch still moves water. The Black Bear and Oriole gold mines are located up Rocky Gulch approximately one mile. The Sordy Mine was a historic placer mining operation. Its location is on private property left bank just prior to the start of Rocky Riffle.

Notes (📖)

There is one osprey nest (○) and a large blue heron rookery (△) in the Douglas-fir trees on the right bank at the end of Rocky Riffle. Talk about squawking. Several times I have seen five or six herons flying around the rookery while being dive-bombed by osprey.

You will frequently see recreational gold miners left bank after you drift past the spot where Rocky Gulch meets the Rogue. It is private property upriver of the gulch on the left bank.

Rocky Riffle Floaters in White Water Action, River Mile 7.1

Floater Identification Question Number 26: Who is this man?

By Michael L. Walker

7.2 RIVER MILE, ROCKY RIFFLE AREA
(▼ ; ⊼)

Just below Rocky Riffle on the left bank is a one-half mile bar that is laced with primitive dirt roads and great dry camp sites. The Rocky Riffle area has a camping limit of three days per week. The access to this camp area is approximately one mile north of the Galice Store on the Galice Highway. No toilets, water, picnic sites, or garbage cans are provided here, just great space.

At this half-way point of our 14-mile float trip you have learned that white water is fun and splashy. It varies between being mild and wild and between being a madcap adventure and a quiet float. I have already checked prior to drifting past the Galice Store Boat Landing that my beer will last. Time for another brewski...an Old English 800 for me!

7.3 RIVER MILE, TWIN ROCKS RIFFLE

Riffle Class and Length (🐟)
Twin Rocks Riffle (#13) is a Class I (0.5) riffle with a drift distance of approximately 200 yards.

How To (💡)
This is another easy riffle. The approach can be recognized by two small guardian rocks right of midriver prior to beginning of the riffle. Follow the "V" slick slightly right of midriver into standing waves. There is a long stretch of slow water at the end of the riffle.

Sloppy Nostalgia (😊)
It can happen anywhere there is slow or flat water, but my last float with my sister, Chris Walker, reminded me of her passion and her excitement at the thought of water fights with the tourists aboard the commercial jet boats. She will try to get you to position the inflatable or ducky right in the path of the jet boat. I am more cautious knowing that the jet boat is much bigger than my craft. In hot weather, the glee she gets from splashing the old, young, healthy, and frail knows no bounds. However, the jet boat nearly always wins in the end by the way the driver positions the jets of the boat. The blast of water from the jets is definitely Class III or IV white water. Five minutes later finds us still bailing.

By Michael L. Walker

Rocky Riffle Floaters, River Mile 7.2

By Michael L. Walker

8.1 RIVER MILE, RED ROCK CUT-BANK

The water here is small and slow, but can be choppy. Your position is below a huge wounded-looking, red cut-bank on the left side of the river next to the Galice Road. Several land slides have occurred here. There is also a boulder-sized red rock in the river left bank just prior to Garden Riffle.

8.3 RIVER MILE, GARDEN RIFFLE

Riffle Class and Length (〰️)

Garden Riffle (#14) is a Class 0.5 riffle with a drift distance of approximately 200 yards. The riffle is named for a garden currently maintained by Norman (Bud) Lewis in the general area where his father, Harry Lewis had lived. Harry was a miner who came to the Galice area in the late 1800's (Grants Pass Courier 1935). The garden is on a bench on the left bank just prior to the riffle. A garden has been at that location for as long as anyone can remember. It can't be seen from the river, but it is visible from the Galice Road.

How To (💡)

This is an easy riffle, just maintain center of "V" slick along the left bank. Right river has shallows and sandpaper. There is a small wave for inflatable kayakers at the beginning of the riffle. Hooks Gulch goes up the mountain on the left bank at the end of this riffle.

8.3 RIVER MILE, HISTORIC ROBERT DEAN PLACER MINE (⛏️)

The land in the big river bend across from the large red cut-bank used to be the Robert Dean Placer Mine and more recently, until purchased by the Bureau of Land Management, was known as the "Pieren Property." The site is a great place to explore a historical hydraulic placer mining operation. Hydraulic mining involved huge nozzles called "hydraulic giants" which forced powerful streams of water against a gravel bar wearing away the gravels. The gravels were then collected and run through sluice boxes. Elaborate ditches and piping systems were developed to collect water under pressure to be forced through the nozzles (Sutton 1966).

The land was patented in 1913 which means it became private property because it was evaluated by the U. S. Government to be a viable mining operation. The U. S. Surveyor General for Oregon stated in mineral survey number 734, "I further certify that Five Hundred Dollars worth of labor has been expended or improvements made upon said Mining Claim by claimants---or their grantors, and that said improvements consist of 1 3/4 miles of Ditch, Value, $2,000.00; Reservoir, Value, $200.00; Hydraulic Giant & Pipe, Value, $200.00; Six Placer excavations, Value, $3,000.00..."

These mining improvements are overgrown with vegetation, but can still be found with little effort. Land your craft right bank after passing through Garden Riffle and walk up an unimproved path to an older time (see Map 8). You will first encounter a flat bench above the river. It is wide and long, and camping is great for small or large groups. A small apple tree marks the site of an old cabin. Follow an old logging/mining road up the gulch and discover history. The largest placer area mined is similar to the type of material associated with the Old Channel Mine. It is well over 100 feet higher than the present river bottom. The mined area has channels, piles of rocks, the probable site of a reservoir, and a few pipe remnants located on a flat bedrock area. This bedrock might mark the historical river bottom of the Rogue River in ancient times.

A solitary heron rookery rests in a single tree on the western-most hill of the old claim (△).

MAP 8
ROBERT DEAN PLACER MINE

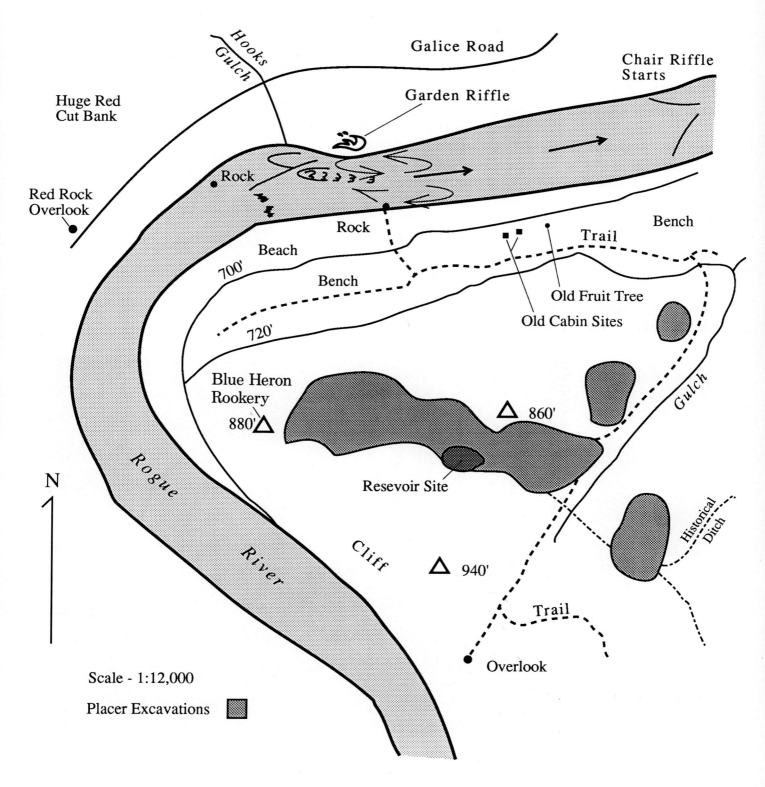

Hooks Gulch

Galice Road

Chair Riffle Starts

Garden Riffle

Huge Red Cut Bank

Rock

Red Rock Overlook

Rock

Beach

700'

Bench

720'

Bench

Trail

Old Fruit Tree

Old Cabin Sites

Blue Heron Rookery

880' △

△ 860'

Resevoir Site

Gulch

N

Rogue

River

Cliff

△ 940'

Historical Ditch

Trail

Overlook

Scale - 1:12,000

Placer Excavations

8.9 RIVER MILE, CHAIR RIFFLE

Riffle Class and Length (🐟)

Chair Riffle (#15) is a Class II (2.0) if the floater runs near right bank, dodges rocks, and hits the cushion. The drift distance is approximately 650 yards (see Diagram 5).

How To (💡)

This riffle is one of the longest on this stretch with the first 350 yards building into the fun part--the next 150 yards of float prior to the cushion. The last 150 yards are anticlimactic after the cushion. Generally, bear midriver for the first two hundred yards at which time you will set up for the two approaches: 1. generally midriver, sneaking left by the rocks with the cushion on right, and 2. right bank for the wildest ride through the rock garden and into the cushion. The rocks prior to the cushion are the closest thing to a rock garden on this stretch and require attentive maneuvering.

The current sweeps into the right bank near the end of this riffle creating a major cushion that the adventurous can run.

Notes (📖)

There is a lonely sentinel boulder left bank on the gravel bar as you pass the cushion. This boulder, supposedly used by Zane Grey while fishing, is shaped like a chair and the reason for the name of this riffle. The last portion of the riffle has standing waves which eventually disappear into flat water.

Chair Riffle's "Sentinel Boulder"

Relaxation Time for Gina and Donnie Above Chair Riffle, River Mile 8.7

By Michael L. Walker

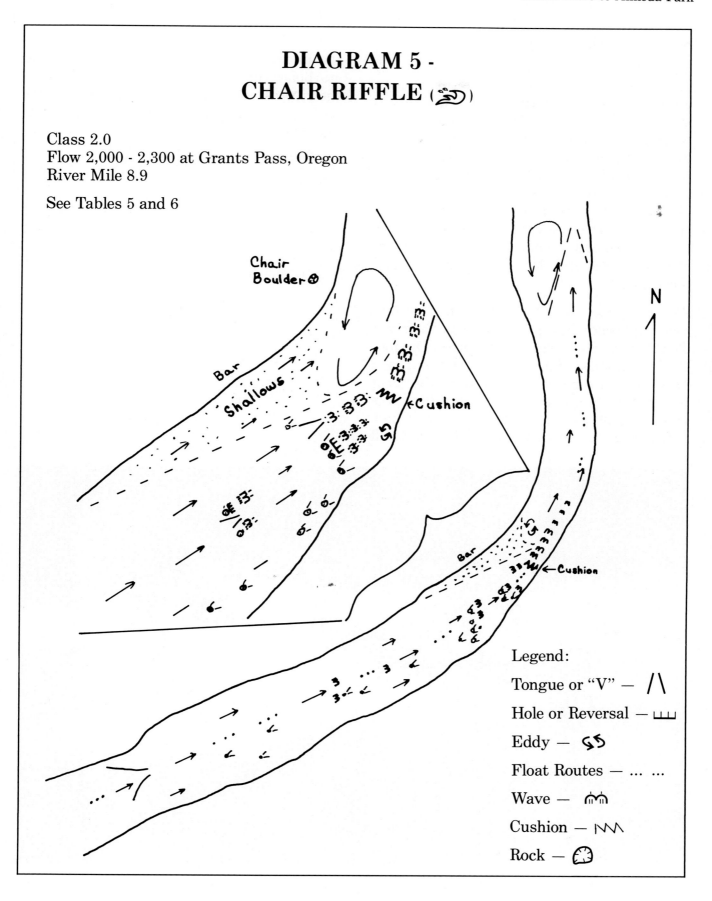

DIAGRAM 5 -
CHAIR RIFFLE

Class 2.0
Flow 2,000 - 2,300 at Grants Pass, Oregon
River Mile 8.9

See Tables 5 and 6

Legend:

Tongue or "V" — /\

Hole or Reversal — ⊔⊔

Eddy — ᏻᏻ

Float Routes — ... ...

Wave — ⌒⌒

Cushion — ⋀⋀⋀

Rock — ⊘

Sloppy Nostalgia (😊)

My sister Chris and I in my Sevytex 375 inflatable found ourselves above the cushion and pushed back to the right bank into a small eddy. The eddy was caused by the billowing water of the cushion that was padding the upriver face of the rocks on the right bank. The extreme turbulence of the cushion was right in front of us, but we were comfortably stationary watching the rest of the floaters in our group sneak the cushion left side. It took me two paddle charges to break through the swift water and churning cushion to head downriver.

Another time two of us were entertaining visiting friends in a paddle raft on the river. The three visitors were from central Oregon, Becky Halstead, Sherrie Skidgel and Linda May. Kurt Emmerich and I were the local boys doing the entertaining. Everything was going fine until we hit the bottom of the Chair Riffle near the cushion, and WHOOSH, all the air exploded out of a three-foot tear in the starboard tube. Becky and Kurt tumbled into the river. I saved the woman by pulling her back into our crippled craft. Kurt kept floating. Smile.

Ducky Floaters Just Above The Cushion of Chair Riffle, River Mile 9.0

By Michael L. Walker

Raft Jam in Cushion of Chair Riffle, River Mile 9.0

By Michael L. Walker

8.9 RIVER MILE, CHAIR RECREATION SITE (▼ ; ✗)

The BLM Chair Recreation Site is a day-use area and has, at this site, a covered picnic table, garbage cans, and parking for approximately six vehicles along with trail access across a bar to the river. Multi-layered river-rock terraces surround the site where the old Kesterson Lodge used to be. I can remember being there for a birthday party during a winter when I was in junior high. I especially remember having fruit salad with strawberries. Strawberries in the middle of winter! I will never forget it. Other remnants of the lodge are fruit trees in what must have been the garden area, and some kind of high-climbing ivy (English Ivy?) imprisoning three ponderosa pine trees up to a height of approximately 50 feet. The diameter of the ivy vines at the base of the trees sometimes reaches as much as two inches.

The Kesterson Lodge was built on a mining claim which was declared to be null and void in 1956. What was unique about the lodge was that the buildings comprising the lodge were valued at approximately $100,000 (USDI 1961 and 1965). "The Kesterson's were well-to-do brothers in the lumber industry, who in 1938 purchased a mining claim located on the banks of the Rogue River, for the sole purpose of having a weekend and summer retreat from pressures of the business world (USDI 1961)."

9.1 RIVER MILE, RAND RECREATION SITE BOAT RAMP

Rand Recreation Site Boat Landing

There is a dirt and gravel road accessing a gravel bar boat launching site (●) and parking for approximately 20 vehicles. The site marks the end of Chair Riffle.

Facilities (✗)

There is no overnight camping at this site as it is a day-use area. No facilities are provided (e.g., garbage cans, toilets, etc.). There is a weather station on site away from the river.

History (■)

Rand used to be a town which some say was named for a mining region in South Africa. The town provided the early miners and trappers with supplies. Later it was a residential area for people who worked in the Almeda Mine and smelter about a mile down river. Even later in the 1930's, Camp Rand housed Civilian Conservation Corps men who were engaged in building roads and bridges (Sutton 1966). The summer of 1987 found it being used as a fire camp for fire fighters fighting the Galice complex wildfire to the west.

By Michael L. Walker

Quiet Area for Floaters Craig and Tom

Notes (📖)

A heron rookery (△) is on the Rand gravel bar with an osprey nest (○) located across the river near the boat landing. A medium-sized madrone and a small pine at the parking area demonstrate the erosional power of the river. Five feet of the madrone's roots are exposed. One-half mile of slow water faces you prior to arriving at Widow Maker (Mark's) Riffle.

Canadian geese with large, white domestic geese companions are usually found here looking for a food hand-out. There is a hard-to-see osprey nest left bank and up high just past the power line (○). If you have been on the river all day and you haven't protected yourself from the sun, you might be turning the color of a crawdad about now.

9.1 RIVER MILE, ASH GULCH

Ash Gulch goes upmountain on the right bank on this slow stretch of the Rogue. It can be identified by a power line swung across the river going to a private residence hidden in the trees near the gulch. The residence is the only private land on the east side of the Rogue downriver from the Hellgate Overlook. It was built by Virgil Hull, of Hull & Hull Funeral Home, Inc., and his sons in 1970 (Murphy 1988).

By Michael L. Walker

9.3 RIVER MILE, RAND VISITORS CENTER (🏠)

Floaters can buy maps and get river information at the Rand Visitor Center. Here is where you pick up your permit to float the wild section of the Rogue during the regulated season. There are steps up the left river bank leading to the Rand Visitor Center. Historically, the visitors' center was the administrative location of the Galice Ranger District from 1934 until 1967, at which time the location was moved to Grants Pass, Oregon. The site was then transferred to the BLM for administration of the Rogue River program.

9.7 RIVER MILE, WIDOW MAKER (MARK'S) RIFFLE

Riffle Class and Length (🦫)

Widow Maker (Mark's) Riffle (#16) is a Class II (1.6) riffle with a drift distance of approximately 400 yards.

How To (💡)

The riffle's first 200 yards captures the action with the last 200 being just a fast drift to the Almeda Park Boat Landing. The river splits at the beginning of the riffle on a large gravel island called Isle and/or Mark's Island. The left flow is shallow and not readily passable. The main "V" of the right flow leads to some fun standing waves, but close to Mark's Island at the riffle entrance you will find a larger wave for the best ride. Next come four separate and distinct rock ledges jutting from the right bank. Unless the water flow is over 1,800 cfs, it is best to work left and avoid the rocks making up the ledges. The first and last ledges are small and you will normally float by them with no problem. The second and third ledges

Do ya wonder what Teresa Donley is doing?

By Michael L. Walker

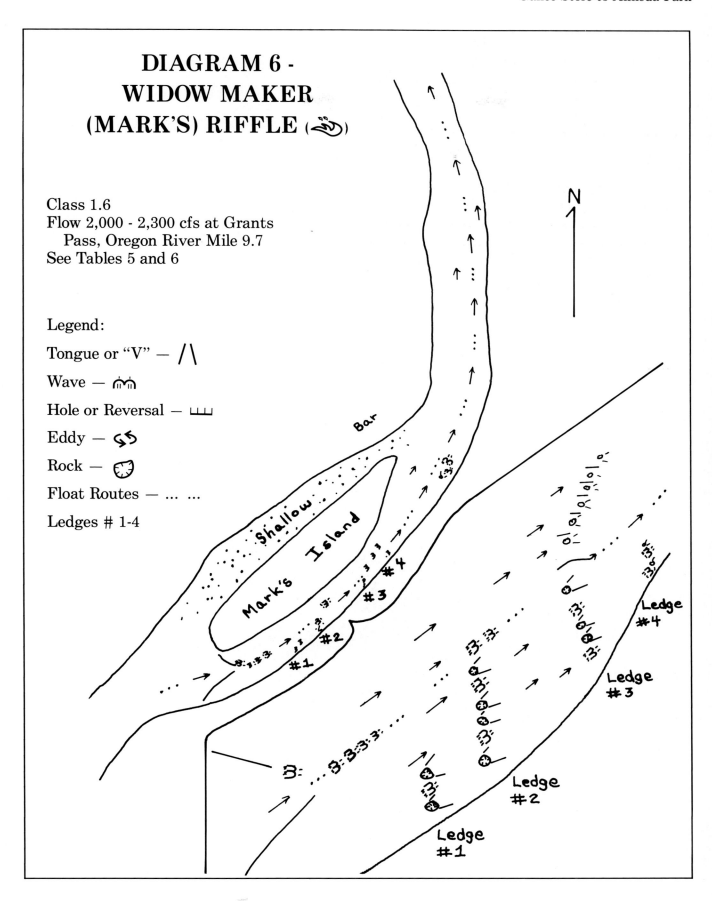

DIAGRAM 6 -
WIDOW MAKER
(MARK'S) RIFFLE

Class 1.6
Flow 2,000 - 2,300 cfs at Grants
   Pass, Oregon River Mile 9.7
See Tables 5 and 6

Legend:

Tongue or "V" — /\

Wave —

Hole or Reversal —

Eddy —

Rock —

Float Routes — ... ...

Ledges # 1-4

N

Bar

Shallow

Mark's Island

#1

#2

#3

#4

Ledge #4

Ledge #3

Ledge #2

Ledge #1

require maneuvering. The river flow will try to push you straight into the second ledge unless you ferry port and skirt the end of the ledge. The third ledge comes soon after and again you should ferry to the port of the main portion threading the middle of the third ledge when it bends and aligns itself with the river. Inflatables can sneak through most of the rocks making up the ledges and play in the waves. Finally the fourth ledge is past and there is one last wave right bank just past the end of Mark's Island (see Diagram 6). Almeda Bar is immediately on the portside following the end of Widow Maker Riffle.

By Michael L. Walker

Floaters at Entrance to Widow Maker Riffle, Going Left of "V" for Best Wave, River Mile 9.7

ALMEDA PARK BOAT LANDING TO GRAVE CREEK BOAT LANDING

Refer to the map entitled "Almeda Park Boat Landing to Grave Creek Boat Landing" for a geographic description of the major points of float interest (see Map 9). This river stretch has a white water index of WW 0.5, an exciting section where riffles occur frequently (see Appendix B).

10.0 RIVER MILE, ALMEDA PARK BOAT LANDING

Almeda Park Boat Landing Description (●)

There is a paved road leading to a concrete boat ramp with parking for approximately 30 vehicles. Except for Argo landing, with a steep gravel access road, floaters who go beyond this point are committed to going the distance to Grave Creek.

Facilities (▲)

Like Indian Mary Park this is another park administered by Josephine County with a full complement of services (except telephone), including year-round improved camping. The park is smaller than Indian Mary Park, but it has an electric air pump for your ducky or inflatable. Use the bulletin board to let your friends know where you are.

Drift Distance (←→) /Time (🕐) To Grave Creek Boat Landing - 4.1 miles/1 to 1 1/4 hours

Sloppy Nostalgia (☺)

Sunday, the celebration of my birthday, August 28, 1988, found us on the Hog Run again. Happily we met "Road Runner" Ed at the Almeda Park Boat Landing for a brief celebration. Road Runner had just completed 700 float miles with his oar-frame raft. Talk about love or fanaticism.

History (⚒ ; ■)

The present day Almeda Park is the location of historical Quartzville and Almeda. Quartzville sputtered briefly in the late 1800's.

Almeda had a post office and a store in the early 1900's. Almeda Park was also used as a fire camp during the summer of 1987. The historic Rand Mine is now located within the park's boundaries.

By Michael L. Walker

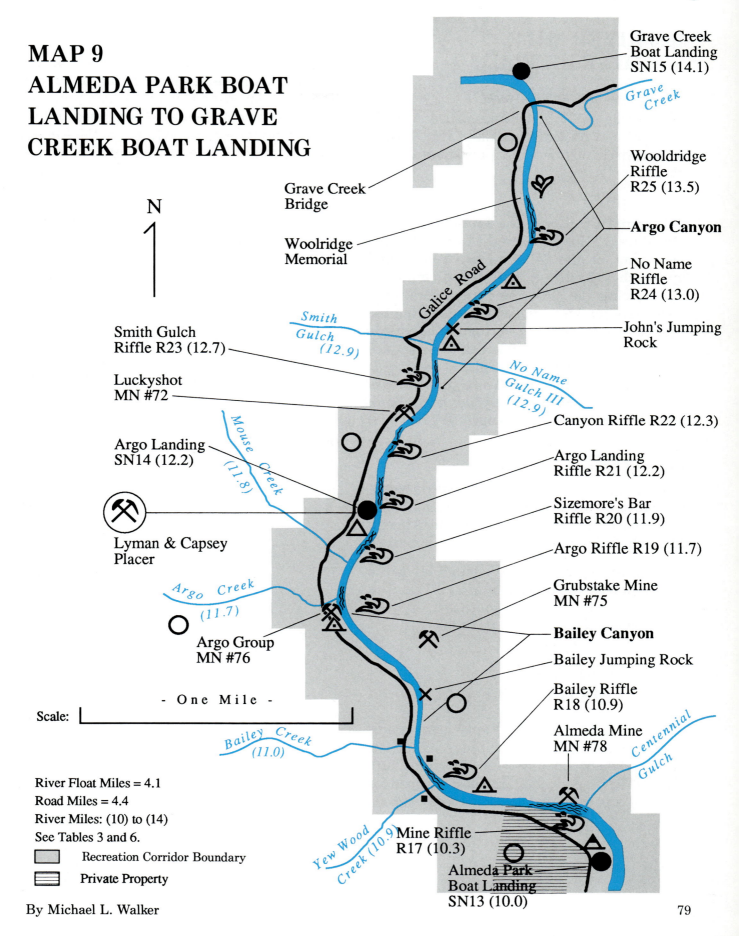

MAP 9
ALMEDA PARK BOAT LANDING TO GRAVE CREEK BOAT LANDING

N

Grave Creek
Boat Landing
SN15 (14.1)

Grave Creek

Wooldridge
Riffle
R25 (13.5)

Argo Canyon

No Name
Riffle
R24 (13.0)

John's Jumping
Rock

Grave Creek
Bridge

Woolridge
Memorial

Galice Road

Smith
Gulch
(12.9)

Smith Gulch
Riffle R23 (12.7)

Luckyshot
MN #72

No Name
Gulch III
(12.9)

Canyon Riffle R22 (12.3)

Argo Landing
SN14 (12.2)

Mouse Creek
(11.8)

Argo Landing
Riffle R21 (12.2)

Sizemore's Bar
Riffle R20 (11.9)

Argo Riffle R19 (11.7)

Lyman & Capsey
Placer

Argo Creek
(11.7)

Grubstake Mine
MN #75

Bailey Canyon

Argo Group
MN #76

Bailey Jumping Rock

Bailey Riffle
R18 (10.9)

- One Mile -

Scale:

Bailey Creek
(11.0)

Almeda Mine
MN #78

Centennial
Gulch

River Float Miles = 4.1
Road Miles = 4.4
River Miles: (10) to (14)
See Tables 3 and 6.

Yew Wood
Creek (10.9)

Mine Riffle
R17 (10.3)

Almeda Park
Boat Landing
SN13 (10.0)

Recreation Corridor Boundary

Private Property

By Michael L. Walker

10.3 RIVER MILE, MINE RIFFLE

Riffle Class and Length (🛶)

Mine Riffle (#17), sometimes called Almeda or Almeda Mine Riffle, is a Class II (2.0) riffle with a drift distance of approximately 450 yards.

How To (💡)

Centennial Creek and the tailings from the old Almeda Mine on the right bank mark the beginning of the Mine Riffle. You should approach the riffle a little left of midriver maintaining the "V." There are several very good standing waves in swift water during the first 200 yards. Near the bottom of the riffle is a major area of hard shell kayak training (see Diagram 7). The approach to this area is between several car-sized boulders. The training area is after the boulders. Catch the eddy right bank and you can play here for hours. Try it, you'll like it!

Notes (📖)

There is a narrow trail about 100 yards before the start of Mine Riffle on the right bank. This short trail leads up to the old Almeda Mine shaft which can be seen from the river.

There is an osprey nest (◯) high up on the left bank near the bottom of Mine Riffle. You can see it while looking southeast on your drift toward the approach to Bailey Riffle.

10.3 RIVER MILE, ALMEDA MINE (⛏)

The Almeda Mine or "Big Yank" ledge is now a ruin of red and yellow tailings and a few hardy relics of machinery on the right bank (Hill 1976; Oregon 1952). It was developed for gold and copper ore and named for Miss Almeda Hand, the niece of the original owner (Sutton 1966). This mine has an existing or current mining claim on it and may still have potential for development one day. There used to be a wooden bridge across the Rogue at the Almeda Mine site until it was washed out by a flood. If you look closely in the sidebank of the Galice Road at this point you will see a lonely one-inch cable embedded in the bank. Walk down to the river just below the bottom of Mine Riffle and you will find a large rock with several one-inch diameter steel bolts embedded in it. These were once used to hold the bridge in place.

The north side of the river below the mine tailings is even more exciting. It reminds me of some moon landscape. The colors, shallow pools, moss, and soil create primordial images in my mind.

History is lying all over this north bank. Rusting machinery is scattered everywhere, especially steel rails.

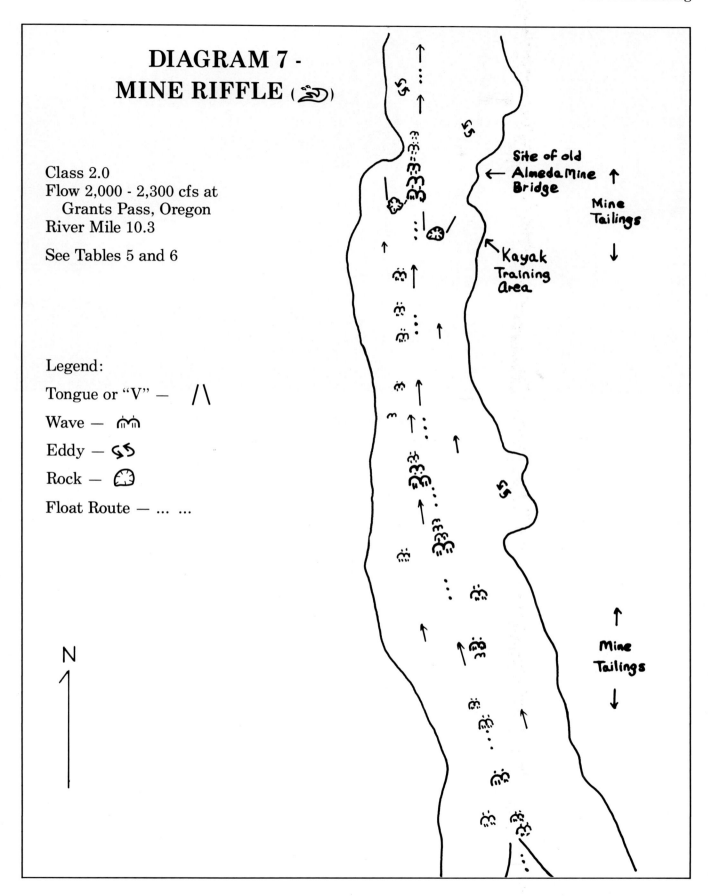

DIAGRAM 7 - MINE RIFFLE

Class 2.0
Flow 2,000 - 2,300 cfs at
   Grants Pass, Oregon
River Mile 10.3

See Tables 5 and 6

Legend:

Tongue or "V" — /\

Wave — ⌒⌒

Eddy — ⌒⌒

Rock — ▱

Float Route — ... ...

N

Site of old
Almeda Mine
Bridge

Mine
Tailings

Kayak
Training
Area

Mine
Tailings

Almeda Mine, River Mile 10.3

By Michael L. Walker

Inflatable Kayakers in Mine Riffle (Lower Stretch), River Mile 10.5

10.9 RIVER MILE, BAILEY RIFFLE

Riffle Class and Length (🦫)

Bailey Riffle (#18) is a Class II (1.8) riffle with a drift distance of approximately 300 yards.

How To (💡)

This riffle starts shortly before Yew Wood Creek enters the Rogue on the left bank. There are two white water areas to this float. Maintain your position in the "V" which is midriver. There is a good standing wave for inflatables at the start of the first white water area, and turbulence and swirls at the end. Stay left of a good-sized rock at the bottom of the first section. This rock sometimes has a great eddy/reversal to catch behind it (see Diagram 8). Catch the eddy when you can and go sun bathing on the rock. Have a beer and wave to the sightseers on the Galice Road. The second part of the riffle starts out with a few small waves with an eddy on the left bank. At higher water there is a hole left bank to hit, otherwise the approach is still midriver through the second set of standing waves. Bailey Creek on the left bank marks the end of this riffle.

Sloppy Nostalgia (😊)

Another tale takes place the summer of 1987 when seven of us each in our own inflatable floated from Carpenter Island Recreation Site to Grave Creek. A flip occurred at the first white water of Bailey Riffle above the eddy caused by the rock at the bottom of the first section. This episode taught us an important river lesson about light keepers. The floater floated and the inflatable stayed at the reversal behind the rock. I don't know how long the inflatable would have stayed stuck in the sticky reversal, but it was there for 15 minutes until we could snag it free and continue our trip.

Hardshell Kayakers in Upper Bailey Riffle, River Mile 10.9

By Michael L. Walker

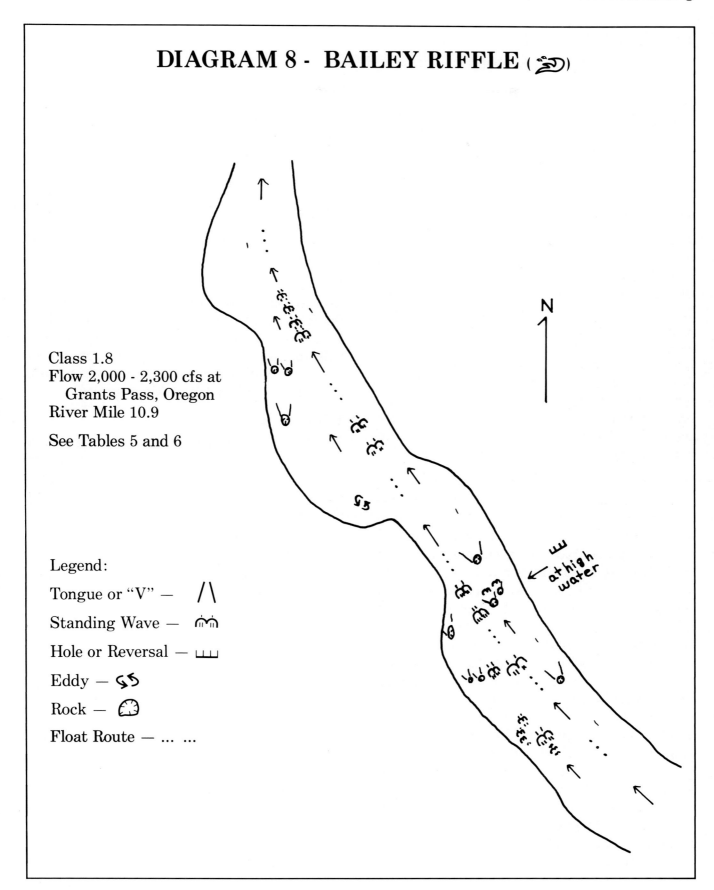

DIAGRAM 8 - BAILEY RIFFLE (🦅)

N

Class 1.8
Flow 2,000 - 2,300 cfs at
    Grants Pass, Oregon
River Mile 10.9

See Tables 5 and 6

at high water

Legend:

Tongue or "V" — /\

Standing Wave — ᗰᗰ

Hole or Reversal — ╙╜

Eddy — ᔕ5

Rock — ⌒

Float Route — ... ...

11.0 RIVER MILE, BAILEY CANYON

Bailey Canyon starts after Bailey Riffle and ends just prior to the beginning of Argo Riffle. This is a slow laid-back section. The drift time to Argo Riffle is slow, taking maybe 15 minutes. The drift distance to Argo Riffle is approximately seven-tenths of a mile.

Sloppy Nostalgia (☺)

There is a large rock on the right bank just into Bailey Canyon called Bailey Jumping Rock (✕). One part of it is used by jumpers and divers as it hangs over a deep portion of the Rogue. The main jumping ledge is 15 feet above the water level with a smaller higher ledge reaching up to 23 feet. The measurements were made the summer of 1988 at a flow of 2,100 cfs at Lost Creek Dam. This is a great spot for large groups to watch the jumpers as the river is wide and deep; there are plenty of places to pull your boat ashore to watch jumpers or climb the rock to jump.

A couple of years ago I was in a small fleet of inflatables and feeling good as we drifted into Bailey Canyon and into a group of floaters who had stopped at Bailey Jumping Rock. I saw a friend, Gail Johnston was her name, and never a more beautiful person. Her husband was jumping off the rock. Gail had been in a terrible automobile accident in her teens which left her paralyzed from the waist down. She was in her wheelchair in the front of a heavy-duty oar raft that day. I went after a great hug as I remembered this gutsy woman. As she also runs this float in a K-79, I asked her one day, "Gail, since your legs don't work, what would you do if your inflatable flipped in fast shallows?" She smiled and explained that she puts floaters on her ankles. I asked, "What kind?" She said, "You know, the kind of floaters that small children wear sometimes on their arms." The floaters would keep her feet up and her bottom off the sharpies. Smile! My kind of woman!

Notes (📖)

There are significant concrete retainer walls supporting the Galice Road up high and close on the left bank.

There is a very small osprey nest (◯) on the top of a large, dead Douglas-fir tree on the right bank prior to Bailey Canyon. Look hard and you may see osprey young in July or August.

If you listen closely in this section you may hear exchanges of "Viking" calls from friendly floating groups who are issuing mild challenges for a water fight. It sounds like: Odennnnnnnnnnnnnn! Best be careful or another Civil War will break out between north-bank and south-bank flotillas. More smiles.

History (■)

The Bradbury or Grubstake Gold Mine (MN # 75) was a lode mine up the hill on the east side of the Rogue in the vicinity of Bailey Creek Canyon. There were three tunnels at elevations 150, 420, and 525 feet above the river level (Oregon 1952).

By Michael L. Walker

The Solitude of Argo Riffle, River Mile 11.7

By Michael L. Walker

Notes

(📖)

A Blank Page for Your Notes

Neil Walker and James Johnson, Mugging for the Camera at Bailey Jumping Rock, River Mile 11.1

By Michael L. Walker

11.7 RIVER MILE, ARGO RIFFLE

Riffle Class and Length (⮆)

Argo Riffle (#19) is a Class II (1.8) riffle with a drift distance of approximately 250 yards. Argo Riffle was considered a falls before Glen Wooldridge blasted it out.

How To (💡)

Argo Creek on the left bank identifies this riffle. Start approach in "V" slick which is right of midriver. Exuberant whoops and wows identify the two very good standing waves during the first third of the run and two large rocks at the bottom of the run. You can float between the rocks or go right of both. These rocks form great inflatable kayaker holes at higher water when the rocks are submerged (see Diagram 9). Your adrenaline should be really flowing as you pass Mouse Creek on the left bank which marks the end of the riffle.

History (■)

The historic Argo Group Gold Mine (MN # 76) was a lode mine located at river level near Argo Creek. Three tunnels, aggregating about 300 feet, were run in on the quartz veins (Diller 1914). A little bit of history is waiting at this historic mining site to delight you.

Notes (📖)

There is an osprey nest (◯) on the left bank high on the ridge near the very beginnings of Argo Creek.

Floaters Charging Argo Riffle, River Mile 11.7

By Michael L. Walker

DIAGRAM 9 - ARGO RIFFLE (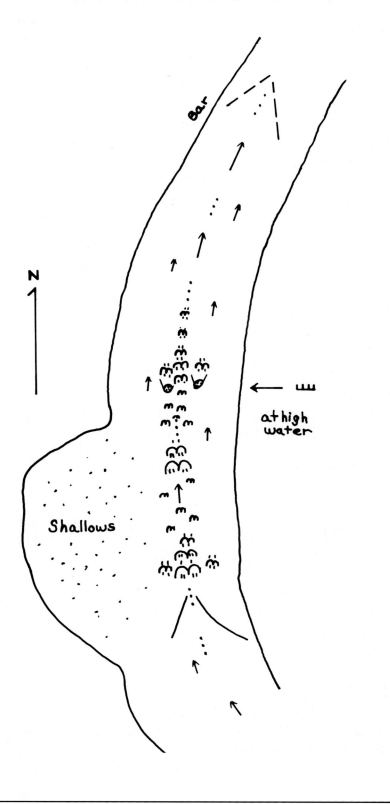)

Class 1.8
Flow 2,000 -2,300 cfs at
  Grants Pass, Oregon
River Mile 11.7

See Tables 5 and 6

Legend:

Tongue or "V" — /\

Wave — 𝖒𝖒

Hole or Reversal — ⊔⊔

Eddy — ⊊⊋

Rock — ⬭

Float Route — ... ...

11.9 RIVER MILE, SIZEMORE'S BAR RIFFLE

Riffle Class and Length (🏊)

Sizemore's Bar Riffle (#20) is a Class I (1.2) riffle with a drift distance of 150 yards. This riffle takes its name from V. O. Sizemore. He had a year-around residence on a mining claim at the Argo Landing bar. The mining claim was valid and went by the name, "Lyman and Capsey Placer." However, Sizemore quit claimed his rights to Josephine County for $5,000.00 and signed an abandonment to the U.S. Government (USDI 1965).

How To (💡)

There is a car-sized rock midriver and diagonal waves from the right bank. No problem, just follow the "V" right of the car-sized rock.

12.2 RIVER MILE, ARGO LANDING (△)

There is a picturesque, steep, narrow, one-vehicle dirt and gravel road winding down to this landing, but there is no boat ramp as such. This is a good dry camp, with a toilet. Your escape from the world continues as you drift by the site.

12.2 RIVER MILE, ARGO LANDING RIFFLE

Riffle Class and Length (🏊)

Argo Landing Riffle (#21) is a Class I (0.8) riffle with a drift distance of approximately 250 yards.

How To (💡)

This is a fun riffle. It is playtime straight through the "V" slick into waves, as long as you miss the large rocks.

12.3 RIVER MILE, CANYON RIFFLE

Riffle Class and Length (🏊)

Canyon Riffle (#22) is a Class I (0.8) riffle with a drift distance of approximately 200 yards.

How To (💡)

You should maintain straight through the "V" slick. There is slow water at the end of this run.

History (■)

Historic Luckyshot Gold Mine (MN # 72) was a lode mine located at river level on the west side of the river just below Canyon Riffle.

Notes (📖)

Another osprey nest (○) hides on the left bank just past Canyon Riffle.

12.5 RIVER MILE, ARGO CANYON

Argo canyon provides some of the most dramatic scenery on the river. It is also dotted with little coves and beaches for picnicking and camping. There are lots of swimming places.

The canyon starts at the end of Canyon Riffle and ends at Grave Creek, close to the takeout. The next two miles after the canyon entrance have no Class II adventures, but the stretch is relatively swift with no major slow water, a solid Class I float. It is the finale of the trip where calendars and clocks are forgotten as you pass between the steep, deep, walls of Argo Canyon. There is no road access and it's a difficult walk-out up steep mountain slopes to the Galice Road on the left bank. Now is not the time to discover that your minimum pre-flight at the Hog Creek put-in missed an air tube leak which casually expands at this time resulting in a sinking ship. Shadows are created by the end of the day within these steep canyon walls.

12.7 RIVER MILE, SMITH GULCH RIFFLE

Riffle Class and Length (✍)

Smith Gulch Riffle (#23) is a Class I (0.8) riffle with a drift distance of approximately 300 yards.

How To (💡)

There are two parts to this riffle. Maintain straight "V" slick through both sections of this riffle. Smith Gulch is on the left bank at the end of the riffle. There is slow water at the end of the run which speeds up five minutes later.

On an easy bend after the end of Smith Gulch Riffle and prior to No Name Riffle, there is another jumping rock. John's Jumping Rock (✗) protrudes slightly from the starboard bank into calm deep water. Its tallest launch spot is 21 feet in the air. Spots to beach your craft and climb the rock are scarce.

13.0 RIVER MILE, NO NAME RIFFLE

Riffle Class and Length (✍)

No Name Riffle (#24) is a Class I (0.5) riffle with a drift distance of approximately 150 yards.

How To (💡)

This is a very easy riffle, just maintain straight through the "V" slick.

13.5 RIVER MILE, WOOLDRIDGE RIFFLE

Riffle Class and Length (✍)

Wooldridge Riffle (#25) is a Class I (1.3) riffle with a drift distance of approximately 450 yards.

How To (💡)

You know Wooldridge Riffle is coming up when you can see the Grave Creek Bridge. There is a submerged rock on the right at the beginning of this float. You should maintain "V" slick left of midriver. There are many rocks right bank that an inflatable can dodge, but generally the first part of this riffle is everyone's run left of midriver. You should bear left until after passing the house-sized rock near the end of the riffle, then bear right. There is a standing wave for inflatables toward the left bank after the house-sized rock.

Sloppy Nostalgia (😊)

The Grave Creek Bridge can be seen in the distance from the approach to Wooldridge Riffle. Its massive concrete structure is quite a contrast to the natural setting into which its supports are embedded. The bridge has become symbolic to me, indicating another successful float trip which, sadly, is at its end. Sometimes, if you're off your schedule, the failing light of late afternoon creates cool shadows you try to avoid as you float on.

The moon has come out. Same old moon, I imagine, that the Rogue Indians must have admired prior to the arrival of the white man. There is little evidence of their passage here with the notable exception of the archaeological diggings downriver at Mule Creek.

At this point I always think of the valley's crazies having successfully conquered the Rogue again at the death of yet another day.

By Michael L. Walker

Beautiful Smith Gulch Riffle, But Can You Find the Rafters? River Mile 12.7

By Michael L. Walker

No Name Riffle, River Mile 13.0

Phil and Mike in Wooldridge Riffle, River Mile 13.6

By Michael L. Walker

Grave Creek Bridge, River Mile 14.0

Inflatable Kayakers in a Hamm's Commercial at Grave Creek Landing, River Mile 14.1

(Mike, Dale, Doug and Alan)

By Michael L. Walker

History (■)

This riffle was named after Glen Wooldridge, easily acknowledged as the father of floating the Rogue. Glen made his first float down the river in 1915. In the 1940's Glen was the first man ever to motor up the Rogue from Gold Beach to Grants Pass (Arman 1982). There is a memorial plaque on stone next to the Galice Road in memory of Glen's love of the river. Glen is gone now but his riffle flows on.

Notes (📖)

There is another osprey nest (◯) on the high canyon walls left bank after Wooldridge Riffle.

14.0 RIVER MILE, GRAVE CREEK BRIDGE (■)

Grave Creek enters the Rogue on the right bank just upriver of the Grave Creek Bridge which spans the river for a distance of 145 feet. There is a small sandy beach right bank at the base of one of the bridge's concrete supports. The water in Grave Creek gets very low in the late summer causing bath-like temperatures in the pools near the mouth of the creek.

A few adventuresome individuals jump from the Grave Creek Bridge on very large rubber bands. They have what looks like a parachute harness which is attached to the top of the bridge with long elastic bands. They jump from the bridge feet first toward the water, traveling almost 100 feet before the elastic bands stretch to the point where they now hurtle back up toward the bottom of the bridge. The speed they are traveling makes the air rush noisily by their hurling bodies. They bounce back and forth for awhile until gravity wins and then, hanging from the bands just above the water, they unhook their harness from the bands and fall into the water. It is quite a sight and sends goose bumps up my spine.

The first Grave Creek Bridge was a 350-foot swinging bridge and was built across the Rogue at Grave Creek by the Civilian Conservation Corps from Camp Rand in 1935 (Sutton 1966). I can remember it creaking and moaning when my father would drive the pickup across it. The swinging bridge became history when it was replaced by today's concrete structure in 1965. Today's bridge is natural habitat for cliff swallows which make their nests in inaccessible spots under the bridge. Spring finds dozens (hundreds?) of them darting around under the bridge.

Your adventure today has almost ended, but you will always cherish the experience. While you take away only your memories, the river will await your return.

By Michael L. Walker

TAKE-OUT: GRAVE CREEK BOAT LANDING

14.1 RIVER MILE, GRAVE CREEK BOAT LANDING (▼)

Landing Description (●)

There is a paved road right down to this concrete boat landing.

Facilities (X)

There are toilets during the summer months and a day-parking area for 15-20 vehicles on-site. Overnight parking occurs off the Galice Road above the landing.

History (■)

Grave Creek took its name in 1846 after a tragic event on its upper reaches near the site of the present-day covered bridge over Grave Creek in Sunny Valley. The event was the death and burial of a young girl, Martha Leland Crowley, traveling with other emigrants from southern Oregon to the Willamette Valley on the old California trail (Grants Pass Courier 1935). Grave Creek is named after her grave.

Sloppy Nostalgia (☺)

This is my last sloppy nostalgia shot, and I miss it already. Plus, there should be more river sections prior to the end. Who designed this handbook anyway?

Well this is the story of an inflatable runner without the proper braces. Yeah, it's about me, Mikie, at that time a reluctant K-79 captain. No, it's not about teeth braces, the kind that make you beautiful. It's about staying in your inflatable through the use of a technique called bracing. I will commit my first and last impropriety by telling a story which did not occur on the Hog Creek Run, but just downriver on the Grave Creek Rapids, a solid Class III float.

My first time floating the wild section of the Rogue would have occurred in the fall of 1981. It was going to be a three-day white water camping trip on the wild section of the Rogue from Grave Creek to Foster Bar. I was going to be a rider in a heavy-duty oar paddle raft.

It rained with the weather gods promising more and the trip was cancelled. On a Saturday, two days later, an impromptu racquetball tournament of those participants who were no longer rafting resulted in an after-tournament beer decision for a one-day float. The float would be 20 miles from Grave Creek to the Rogue River Ranch. There is no road access to the river at the Rogue River Ranch (originally Marial) at the end of our float, but it's just a 15-20 minute hike uphill with your deflated inflatable on your back to the Marial Road and your link back home (it feels like a long link).

My first descent into Grave Creek Rapid in a K-79 was exciting. I was a little afraid to float it, but at the same time I wanted to do it more than I didn't. I charged and crashed, the same as the Dunn Riffle story, and except for enthusiasm, another poor show. My friend and river mentor, Bill Gasow, a hard-shell kayaker on the trip with me, and Burl Owens, a novice hard-shell kayaker and I talked after I purged my mouth of water. Bill, smiling, asked a simple question, "Mike (he did not know I was Mikie), do you know what bracing is?" I laughingly said, "Is that something I should have on my teeth?" Bill now laughing said, "No, but let me tell you." Another lesson was learned which is applicable to the Hog Run. You don't save an inflatable the same way you save a ducky from a flip. Paddle bracing is applicable to hard shell and inflatable kayakers. If you are flipping you do not go to the high side, a technique which will save you in a ducky. What you should do is paddle charge the low side which forces the low tube of the inflatable back up to a stable position. What an exciting lesson! I flipped in the very first rapid of the wild section, but with that advice I made it to the Rogue River Ranch with only bailing as a chore. On our trip home, Bill, still smiling, said that after my first flip he thought it was going to be a long day. Happily his advice worked and I endured only the right kind of heart pounding from then on.

Notes (📖)

Don't miss this landing. The next official take-out is 35 miles down the river at Foster Bar. There is also road access with a small hike at the Bureau of Land Management Rogue River Ranch 20 miles down the river (USDA/USDI). Remember, floating the wild section from June 1st through September 15th is by **permit only**. Permits should be sought through the Rand Visitor Center.

The Grave Creek Boat Landing is where your shuttle vehicle(s) should be to take you back to Hog Creek and your transportation home. You could go east on the Grave Creek Road to Leland and the I-5 highway at Sunny Valley and the historic Grave Creek covered bridge.

Trail To Foster Bar (■)

A national trail starts here on the right bank of the Rogue. It goes through the entire wild section of the Rogue. Approximately three miles down this trail is the historic Whiskey Creek Cabin. Today it is on the National Register of Historic Places, and it is the oldest known standing mining cabin in the remote wild section of the Rogue. The cabin and surrounding area remain isolated and inaccessible except by river or trail, much like it was when early pioneers first inhabited the area.

Trail To Rainie Falls

On the left bank near the concrete bridge another trail starts. It is well maintained to Rainie Falls, a Class VI rapid. It is one and one-half miles to the falls for a great, short day hike. It is primarily used by fishermen, but more and more sightseers are using it, especially during the season when it's good for viewing jumping salmon.

"The river is for you, the macho hearted girl or boy, man or woman. The shine in your eyes tells if you are qualified." (Mikie Walker 1988)

TABLE 1 - GOLD MINES[1] (⚒)

Mine Name		Mineralization Type	Located On
MN-69.	Prospect	- - - - - - - - - -	Rogue River
MN-71.	Legal Tender Group	Quartz Vein	Argo Gulch
MN-72.	Lucky Shot*	Quartz Vein	Rogue River
MN-73.	Scandinavian-American	Stream Channel	Bailey Gulch
MN-74.	Seven Thirty (Juanita)	Volcanogenic	Argo Creek
MN-75.	Bradbury (Grubstake)*	Quartz Vein	Rogue River
MN-76.	Argo Group*	Quartz Vein	Rogue River
MN-77.	Independence	Volcanogenic	Rocky Gulch
MN-78.	Almeda*	Volcanogenic	Rogue River
MN-79.	Golden Wedge	Quartz Vein	Bailey Creek
MN-81.	Rocky Gulch (Kramer)	Quartz Vein	Rocky Gulch
MN-82.	Richmond Group	Quartz Vein	Bailey Creek
MN-83.	Sordy	Quartz Vein	Rocky Gulch
MN-84.	Rand*	Placer	Rogue River
MN-91.	Mayflower Group	Quartz Vein	Rocky Gulch
MN-92.	Black Bear	Quartz Vein	Rocky Gulch
MN-93.	Oriole	Quartz Vein	Rocky Gulch
MN-95.	Robert Dean Placer*	Placer	Rogue River
MN-96.	Prospect (name unknown)	Quartz Vein	Rich Gulch
MN-97.	Spokane Group	Quartz Vein	Rich Gulch
MN-98.	Last Chance	Placer	Rocky Gulch
MN-99.	Old Channel	Placer	Rich Gulch
MN100.	Sordy (Golden Eagle)*	Placer	Rogue River
MN100a.	Rocky Gulch	Placer	Rocky Gulch
MN101.	Victor	Quartz Vein	Galice Creek
MN102.	Nesbit Group	Volcanogenic	Galice Creek
MN136.	Strenuous Teddy	Hydrothermal	Galice Creek
MN137.	Gold Plate	Quartz Vein	Galice Creek
MN138.	Sugar Pine	Quartz Vein	Galice Creek
MN139.	Golden Pheasant Group	Quartz Vein	Galice Creek
MN140.	Golden Bar	Placer	Galice Creek
MN141.	Cal-Ore (Old Dan Green)	Placer	Galice Creek
MN142.	Liepold	Placer	Galice Creek
MN144.	Hansen	Quartz Vein	Galice Creek
MN145.	Lost Flat	Quartz Vein	Galice Creek
MN146.	Yankee Chief Group	Placer	Galice Creek
MN148.	Fowler Group	Placer	Galice Creek
MN149.	Stratton Creek*	Placer	Stratton Creek
MNXXX.	Hellgate Placer*	Placer	Rogue River

1. These historical mines are on or near tributaries of the Rogue River from Hog Creek to Grave Creek (see Ramp and Peterson 1979). The mines identified with an asterisk (*) are within the recreation corridor of the Rogue River. Interested people should contact the Bureau of Land Management and check the land status when pursuing recreational gold mining.

By Michael L. Walker

TABLE 2 - FLOODS[1] (■)

Year	Date	Peak Discharge (cfs) [2,3]	Gauge Height (feet) [3]
1853 [4]	-- -- --	--,---	--.--
1861	12/--/61	175,000	42.00
1890	-- -- --	160,000	35.00
1903	01/29/03	--,---	35.00
1907	02/ -- /07	60,500	--.--
1909	11/ -- /09	70,000	--.--
1927 [5]	02/ -- /27	138,000	31.00
1942	12/ -- /42	34,400	--.--
1945	12/29/45	70,000	23.16
1948	01/07/48	59,900	21.06
1950	10/29/50	65,400	21.25
1953	01/18/53	77,000	23.90
1953	11/23/53	66,000	21.15
1955	12/22/55	135,000	29.60
1958	01/29/58	63,200	21.24
1962	12/02/62	99,800	27.30
1964 [6]	12/23/64	152,000	34.15
1971	03/02/71	82,500	23.20
1972	01/22/72	80,500	23.07
1981	12/20/81	78,700	22.89
1983	02/18/83	73,300	22.88

19 Floods

1. Flood measurements are on the Rogue River at Grants Pass, Oregon. The River Forecast Center of the National Weather Service works in conjunction with the Corps of Engineers to determine the elevation of "flood stage," which has been determined to be 20 feet at Grants Pass, Oregon. The above information for the years 1945 to 1983 was received by the author from the U. S. Geological Survey December 8, 1987. Gauge height for the floods of 1861, 1890, and 1927 are recorded in U. S. Geological Survey Open-file Report 84-454 (also see Oregon 1959; Hill 1976).

2. For a comparison, 2,269 cubic feet per second (cfs) was the average monthly flow at Grants Pass, Oregon during June, July, and August, 1985 (see Table 5). It was 2,179 cfs for the same period in 1986.

3. The relationship between cfs and feet is not permanent and changes over time (see Graph 4).

4. The first recorded flood in Josephine County was in 1853 (Sutton 1966).

5. Original Hellgate Bridge built in 1913 was destroyed in the 1927 flood (Hill 1976). Prior to 1913 all traffic into the Galice area was across a ferry.

6. Second Hellgate Bridge damaged and later replaced by the third and present Hellgate Bridge (Sutton 1966).

By Michael L. Walker

TABLE 3 - DISTANCES & FLOAT TIMES[1]

DISTANCES (↔)

Distances in Miles Between Selected Communities/Boat Landings in southern Oregon (see Map One - Road Trip and Shuttle)

Communities/ Boat Landing	Almeda	Ashland	Ennis Riffle	Galice	Grants Pass	Grave Creek	Hog Creek	Indian Mary Park	Medford	Merlin	Wolf Creek
Almeda	00	66	06	04	26	04	12	10	56	16	33
Ashland	66	00	60	59	40	68	63	54	10	47	67
Ennis Riffle	06	60	00	02	20	10	07	04	50	12	26
Galice	04	59	02	00	19	08	09	07	49	14	29
Grants Pass	26	40	20	19	00	28	13	14	30	07	27
Grave Creek	04	68	10	08	28	00	15	14	58	21	38
Hog Creek	12	63	07	09	13	15	00	03	53	05	23
Indian Mary Park	10	54	04	07	14	14	03	00	44	08	26
Medford	57	10	50	49	30	58	53	44	00	37	57
Merlin	16	47	12	14	07	21	05	08	37	00	18
Wolf Creek	33	67	26	29	27	38	23	26	57	18	00

FLOAT TIMES [1] (🕐)

Float Times (approximate) in Hours Between Major Boat Landings

The following approximate float times are based on a straight-through float without stopping (i.e., no water fights, wildlife viewing, rock climbing, or diving/jumping) and moderate paddling through the slow stretches at a river flow varying from 1,500 cubic feet per second (cfs) to 2,300 cfs (see Map Two - Rogue River: Hog Creek to Grave Creek).

1. Hog Creek Boat Landing to Indian Mary Park Boat Landing . . . . 0.75 - 1.00 hours
2. Indian Mary Park Boat Landing to Ennis Riffle Boat Landing . . . . 1.00 - 1.25 hours
3. Ennis Riffle Boat Landing to Galice Store Boat Landing . . . . 0.75 - 1.00 hours
4. Galice Store Boat Landing to Almeda Park Boat Landing . . . . 1.00 - 1.25 hours
5. Almeda Park Boat Landing to Grave Creek Boat Landing . . . . 1.00 - 1.25 hours

Totals . . . . 4.50 - 5.75 hours

1. Distances are from selected communities in southern Oregon; float times are between major boat landings from Hog Creek to Grave Creek on the Rogue River.

TABLE 4 - MONTHLY FLOW [1]

Mean Monthly River Flow in cubic feet per second (cfs) for Selected Communities or Locations on the Rogue River

Communities [2] Locations	----- 1984 -----							----------- 1985 -----------				
	OCT	NOV	DEC	JAN	FEB	MAR	APR	MAY	JUN	JUL	AUG	SEP
McLeod	1422	3544	2384	1393	1195	1162	3393	2469	2267	2164	2255	1757
Grants Pass	1875	7669	5126	2554	3364	2318	5411	2810	2410	2093	2304	2079
Agness	2512	16650	8780	3949	6334	4316	7656	3828	3147	2397	2412	2374

Daily Extremes for Year 1985

McLeod:	Maximum	6,400 cfs,	November 13
	Minimum	927 cfs,	February 4
Grants Pass:	Maximum	23,300 cfs,	November 12
	Minimum	1,220 cfs,	June 20
Agness:	Maximum	51,000 cfs,	November 28
	Minimum	1,820 cfs,	September 29-30

Daily Extremes for Recorded Years

McLeod: Years 1965 - 1985
           Maximum   30,000 cfs,   March 3, 1972
           Minimum   604 cfs,   September 5, 1968

Grants Pass: Years 1938 - 1985
           Maximum 152,000 cfs,   December 23, 1964
           Minimum   606 cfs,   September 10, 1968

Agness: Years 1960 - 1985
           Maximum 290,000 cfs,   December 23, 1964
           Minimum   608 cfs,   July 9-10, 1968

1. See Alexander et al. 1987.

2. McLeod is a gauging station on the Rogue River downriver from Casey Park, and Agness is downriver of the wild section of the Rogue.

By Michael L. Walker

TABLE 5 - DAILY FLOW[1]

Cubic Feet per Second (cfs) and Water Level in Feet

Day	June cfs	June feet	July cfs	July feet	August cfs	August feet	September cfs	September feet
1	3430	(3.38)	1820	(2.17)	2420	(2.68)	2360	(2.64)
2	3400	(3.35)	1910	(2.29)	2400	(2.69)	2520	(-.--)
3	3270	(3.31)	1890	(2.25)	2330	(2.64)	2560	(2.81)
4	2820	(3.30)	1890	(2.26)	2300	(2.73)	2490	(2.73)
5	2800	(2.99)	1930	(2.30)	2300	(2.58)	2470	(2.73)
6	2590	(2.80)	1930	(2.30)	2250	(2.58)	2490	(2.72)
7	2640	(2.81)	1890	(2.26)	2210	(2.50)	2560	(2.76)
8	2800	(2.93)	1900	(2.28)	2230	(2.55)	2590	(2.82)
9	3200	(3.22)	2050	(2.41)	2250	(2.53)	2710	(2.88)
10	3100	(3.19)	2130	(2.46)	2290	(2.60)	2850	(3.03)
11	2970	(3.08)	2150	(2.50)	2330	(2.60)	2770	(3.03)
12	2770	(2.98)	2160	(2.50)	2300	(2.58)	2630	(2.90)
13	2540	(2.89)	2200	(2.50)	2250	(2.58)	2370	(2.71)
14	2550	(2.82)	2180	(2.50)	2270	(2.58)	2220	(2.61)
15	2520	(2.75)	2190	(2.52)	2280	(2.59)	1980	(2.41)
16	2510	(2.77)	2160	(2.52)	2260	(2.56)	1700	(2.18)
17	2500	(2.77)	2140	(2.46)	2270	(2.56)	1690	(2.11)
18	2130	(2.55)	2160	(2.47)	2300	(2.59)	1730	(2.11)
19	1960	(2.43)	2130	(2.49)	2390	(2.66)	1770	(2.15)
20	1770	(2.22)	2110	(2.45)	2370	(2.67)	1760	(2.15)
21	1820	(2.21)	2130	(2.45)	2400	(2.69)	1740	(2.15)
22	1790	(2.14)	2120	(2.46)	2350	(2.68)	1730	(2.10)
23	1780	(2.14)	2120	(2.46)	2330	(2.63)	1690	(2.12)
24	1820	(2.19)	2180	(2.49)	2320	(2.63)	1600	(2.08)
25	1760	(2.11)	2170	(2.50)	2290	(2.62)	1590	(2.01)
26	1810	(2.20)	2150	(2.50)	2300	(2.62)	1570	(1.99)
27	1810	(2.20)	2170	(2.47)	2250	(2.59)	1550	(1.97)
28	1800	(2.16)	2160	(2.50)	2290	(2.59)	1560	(1.97)
29	1810	(2.17)	2230	(2.54)	2300	(2.62)	1560	(1.97)
30	1820	(2.20)	2250	(2.59)	2280	(2.62)	1560	(1.95)
31	----	(----)	2290	(2.61)	2320	(2.60)	----	(1.97)
Total	72290	(80.30)	64890	(75.50)	71430	(80.90)	62370	(71.80)
Mean	2410	(2.70)	2093	(2.40)	2304	(2.60)	2079	(2.40)
Max.	3430	(3.38)	2290	(2.61)	2420	(2.68)	2850	(3.03)
Min.	1760	(2.20)	1820	(2.17)	2210	(2.50)	1550	(1.97)

1. The daily summer flow is for Grants Pass, Oregon on the Rogue River in 1985. See Alexander et al. 1987 for cfs data and the Grants Pass Water Filtration Plant monthly operating report records for water level in feet data.

By Michael L. Walker

TABLE 6 - RIFFLES[1]

River Mile	Riffle Number	Name of Riffle	Length (yards)	Class [2]	Elevation (feet)
0.0	N/A	Hog Creek Put-in	N/A	N/A	756
0.1	R1	Hog Riffle	400	0.6	755
0.7	R2	Dunn Riffle	400	2.2 [3]	750
1.2	R3	Hellgate Riffle	300	1.3 [4]	730
1.4	R4	Bridge Riffle	200	0.5	725
2.6	R5	Indian Riffle	400	0.5	723
3.0	R6	Massie Riffle	200	0.5	720
3.5	R7	Taylor Creek Riffle	200	0.7	716
3.8	R8	Old Man Riffle	300	0.5	714
4.8	R9	Ennis Riffle	600	1.4	710
5.9	R10	Galice Chute Riffle	600	2.0 [5]	700
6.6	R11	Galice Store Riffle	300	2.0 [6]	690
7.1	R12	Rocky Riffle	300	1.0	687
7.3	R13	Twin Rocks Riffle	200	0.5	681
8.3	R14	Garden Riffle	200	0.5	673
8.9	R15	Chair Riffle	650	2.0 [7]	667
9.7	R16	Widow Maker Riffle	400	1.6	663
10.3	R17	Mine Riffle	450	2.0	655
10.9	R18	Bailey Riffle	300	1.8	645
11.7	R19	Argo Riffle	250	1.8	630
11.9	R20	Sizemore's Bar Riffle	150	1.2	628
12.2	R21	Argo Landing Riffle	250	0.8	625
12.3	R22	Canyon Riffle	200	0.8	624
12.7	R23	Smith Gulch Riffle	300	0.8	621
13.0	R24	No Name Riffle	150	0.5	619
13.5	R25	Wooldridge Riffle	450	1.3	617
14.1	N/A	Grave Greek Take-out	N/A	N/A	610
14.1 Miles	25 Riffles		150 to 1,000	0.5 to 2.2	146 foot change

1. Riffles are on the Rogue River from Hog Creek to Grave Creek (see Maps 2 through 9).

2. Riffle class is for a flow approximating 1,900 to 2,200 cubic feet per second (cfs). If the water temperature is below 50 degrees fahrenheit the riffles should be considered one class more difficult (see Appendix B).

3. Riffle is Class II (2.2) if floater hits main reversal.

4. Riffle is Class I (1.4) if floater hits upper hole.

5. Riffle is Class II (2.0) if floater hits reversal.

6. Riffle is Class II (2.0) if floater hits main hole.

7. Riffle is Class II (2.0) if floater runs near right bank and hits cushion.

By Michael L. Walker

TABLE 7 - CREEKS AND GULCHES[1]

River Mile	Name of Creek of Gulch	Type
0.0	Hog Creek	Perennial
0.6	Zigzag Creek	Intermittent
0.7	Little Zigzag Creek	Intermittent
0.7	No Name Gulch I - Right Bank	Intermittent
2.4	Blue Canyon	Intermittent
2.6	No Name Gulch II - Right Bank	Intermittent
3.0	Stratton Creek	Perennial
3.5	Taylor Creek	Perennial
4.2	Paine Gulch	Intermittent
5.9	Spangler Gulch	Intermittent
6.0	Galice Creek	Perennial
7.0	Rich Gulch	Intermittent
7.1	Rocky Gulch	Perennial
7.3	Maple Gulch	Intermittent
8.3	Hooks Gulch	Intermittent
8.7	Belknap Gulch	Intermittent
9.4	Ash Gulch	Intermittent
10.2	Centennial Gulch	Intermittent
10.9	Yew Wood Creek	Perennial
11.0	Bailey Creek	Perennial
11.7	Argo Creek	Perennial
11.8	Mouse Creek	Perennial
12.9	No Name Gulch III - Right Bank	Perennial
12.9	Smith Gulch	Intermittent
14.0	Grave Creek	Perennial

| 14 Miles | 25 Creeks/Gulches | |

1. The identified creeks and gulches are on the Rogue River from Hog Creek to Grave Creek (see USGS 1946; Oregon 1959 and 1970). Also see Maps 2 through 9.

TABLE 8 - LOSS OF LIFE[1]

(1980 through 1988)

River Mile	Location	Year	Accident	Wearing Life Vest
0.2	Hellgate Canyon	1980's	Death	No
0.2	Hellgate Canyon	1984	Death	No
0.2	Hellgate Canyon	1985	Death	No
0.7	Dunn Riffle	1983	Death	No
0.7	Dunn Riffle	Unknown [2]	Death	?
3.5	Taylor Creek Riffle	1984	Death	No
3.8	Old Man Riffle	1981	Death	No
6.6	Galice Store Riffle	1985	Death	No
9.7	Widow Maker Riffle	1986	Death	No

9 Fatalities

1. The "Loss of Life" table represents drownings on the Rogue River from Hog Creek to Grave Creek. This list of accidents reflects the available records of the Sheriff of Josephine County, the Oregon State Marine Board, and the Grants Pass Courier Publishing Company. Thanks to Mary Bradford, the librarian.

Almost 30 people die each year in Oregon while boating recreationally (State Marine Board). This includes boating of all types from motorized boating in the Pacific Ocean to boating in rivers, lakes, and bays. Marty Law of the State Marine Board refers to the "...85% solution to fatal boat accidents. In other words, 85% of all boating fatalities would have been prevented had the victims worn a life vest."

"In an average year, six to ten people die in canoeing and rafting accidents in the State of Oregon" (State Marine Board). There are no known fatalities of individuals on the Rogue River from Hog Creek to Grave Creek when wearing a life vest. Three of the ten fatalities identified for the Hog run were reported to be associated with the consumption of alcohol. Available records identified 32 (30 male and two female) fatalities for the upper Rogue River and it tributaries. The average age was 29 years old. Only one individual was wearing a life vest when he drowned.

2. Dunn Riffle is supposedly named for a person named Dunn who drowned in the riffle.

TABLE 9 - (△ ; △ ; ●)
PARKS/WAYSIDES/ACCESS[1]

River Mile	Site Number	Site Name (SN)	RA	BL	P	T	PT	C	PH	WC
0.0	SN1	Hog Creek Boat Landing	x	x	x	x				x
1.4	SN2	Hellgate Bridge	x		x					
1.7	SN3	Stratton Creek Recreation Site	x		x	x	x			x
2.5	SN4	Indian Mary Park Boat Landing	x	x	x	x	x	IC	x	x
2.9	SN5	Rainbow Recreation Site	x		x	x	x			x
4.7	SN6	Ennis Boat Landing	x	x	x	x				x
5.9	SN7	Carpenter's Island Recreation Site	x		x		x			x
6.8	SN8	Galice Store	x	x	x	x			x	x
7.4	SN9	Rocky Riffle Area	x		x			DC		
8.9	SN10	Chair Recreation Site	x		x		x			x
9.1	SN11	Rand Recreation Site	x	x	x					
9.3	SN12	Rand Visitor Center	x		x	x			x	
10.0	SN13	Almeda Park	x	x	x	x	x	IC		x
12.2	SN14	Argo Landing	x		x	x		DC		
14.1	SN15	Grave Creek Boat Landing	x	x	x	x				x

1. Parks, waysides, and access on the Rogue River from Hog Creek to Grave Creek (see Maps 2 through 9).

Legend

RA = River Access
BL = Boat Landing (●)
P = Parking
T = Toilet
PT = Picnic Table
C = Camping
IC = Improved Camping (△)
DC = Dry Camp/Road Access (△)
PH = Phone
WC = Waste Cans

By Michael L. Walker

TABLE 10 - WILDLIFE[1]

Birds

Great Blue Heron (△)
Osprey (○)
Common Merganser (duck)
Killdeer
Cliff Swallow
Canada Geese
Domestic Geese
Vulture
Woodpecker

Fish

Steelhead
Trout
Eel
Carp
Salmon

Mammals

Otter
Gray Digger (squirrel)
Black-Tailed Deer
Beaver
Mink
Skunk
Chipmunk
Porcupine
Black Bear

Reptiles

Turtle
Water Snake
Rattlesnake
Blue Racer Lizard
Alligator Lizard
Frog

Great Blue Heron

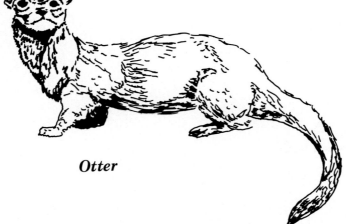

Otter

1. The wildlife list represents critters the author has personally seen on the Rogue River from Hog Creek to Grave Creek. There are many other species of wildlife here (e.g., raccoon, puma, etc.).

By Michael L. Walker

TABLE 11 - WATER TEMPERATURE[1]

MAXIMUM TEMPERATURES ( )

"Maximum" Water Temperature (fahrenheit) for Selected Communities or Locations on the Rogue River

Communities[2] Locations	YEARS/MONTHS											
	----- 1984 -----			--------------------					1985	--------------		
	OCT	NOV	DEC	JAN	FEB	MAR	APR	MAY	JUN	JUL	AUG	SEP
McLeod	46	46	44	42	42	44	48	54	58	57	54	54
Grants Pass	55	47	44	44	46	50	56	63	69	69	67	63
Agness	60	--	46	45	48	53	--	--	--	77	73	65

MINIMUM TEMPERATURES ( )

"Minimum" Water Temperature for Selected Communities or Locations on the Rogue River

Communities/ Locations	YEARS/MONTHS											
	----- 1984 -----			--------------------					1985	--------------------		
	OCT	NOV	DEC	JAN	FEB	MAR	APR	MAY	JUN	JUL	AUG	SEP
McLeod	44	42	41	39	39	40	44	46	52	54	48	44
Grants Pass	45	40	37	36	36	39	46	50	55	60	56	52
Agness	48	--	40	39	39	42	--	--	--	67	63	58

1. See Alexander et al. 1987.

2. McLeod is a gauging station on the Rogue River downriver from Casey Park, and Agness is downriver of the wild section of the Rogue.

GRAPHS

GRAPH 1 - RIFFLE DIFFICULTY[1]

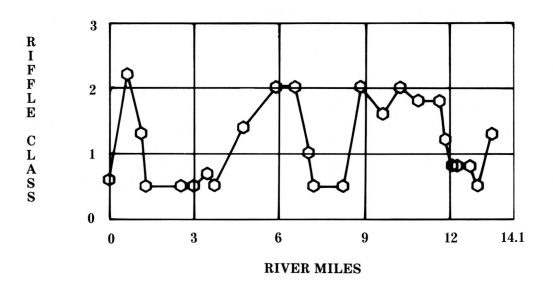

GRAPH 2 - TEMPERATURE'S EFFECT ON RIFFLE DIFFICULTY[1]

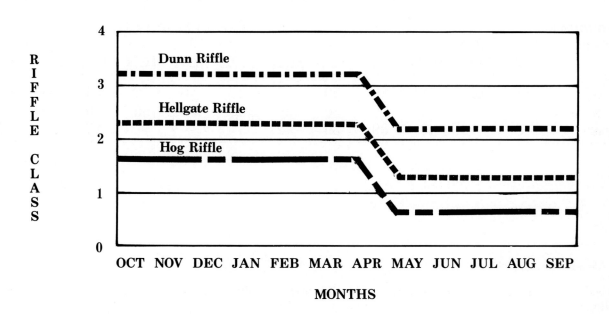

1. The graphs are for a section of the Rogue River between Hog Creek and Grave Creek. Graph 1 is the riffle difficulty for all 25 riffles (see Table 6) when the temperature of the river water is above 50 degrees fahrenheit (F). Graph 2 is an example of how the difficulty classification of three riffles changes over the seasons when the minimum average monthly water temperature dips below 50 degrees F (see Table 11).

By Michael L. Walker

GRAPH 3 - MONTHLY FLOW[1]

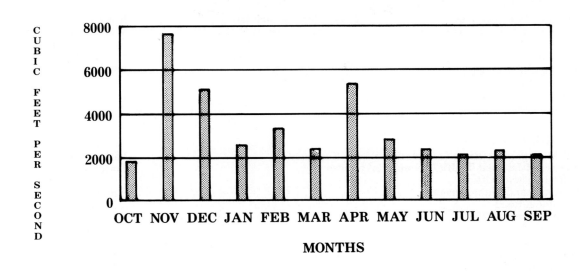

GRAPH 4 - RELATIONSHIP OF CFS AND FEET MEASUREMENTS[1]

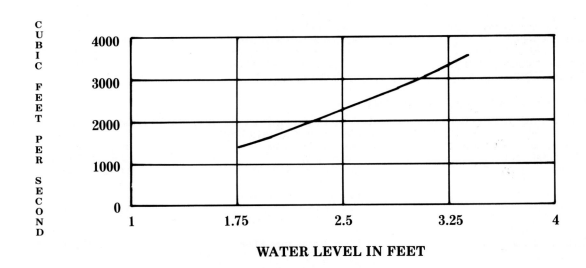

1. Graph 3 is for monthly flow on the Rogue River at Grants Pass, Oregon in 1984-1985 (see Table 4). Graph 4 indicates the relationship between cubic feet per second (cfs) and feet measurements for the Rogue River at Grants Pass in 1985 (see Table 5). This relationship changes with the changes in the river channel (USDI 1985).

APPENDIX A
ADDITIONAL INFORMATION

I. TELEPHONES FOR FLOW AND TEMPERATURE CONDITIONS

River Out-Flow (cfs) and
Temperature at Lost Creek Dam
Corps of Engineers
1 (800) 472-2434

River Flow (cfs & feet)
at Grants Pass
Water Filtration Plant
(503) 474-6353

River Flow (cfs and feet)
and Temperature at Grants Pass
Radio Station KAGI/Copeland
Paving Sand and Gravel
Weather Forecast
(503) 479-4229

River Flow (cfs and feet) and
Water Temperature at Grants Pass
Skipper's Fishing Tackle
Merlin, Oregon
(503) 479-2534

II. AGENCIES

Land Management/River Information/Scenic Easements
Commercial Jet Boat Traffic/Commercial Guides
Medford District Office
Bureau of Land Management
3040 Biddle Road
Medford, Oregon 97504
(503) 770-2275

River Information
Rand Visitor Center
River Permits/Information
14335 Galice Road
Merlin, Oregon 97531
(503) 479-3735

Camp Fires
Forestry Department
State of Oregon
5286 Table Rock Road
Central Point, Oregon 97502
(503) 664-3328

State Dredging/Noise
Dept. Environmental Quality
State of Oregon
811 SW Sixth Avenue
Portland, Oregon 97204-1390
(503) 229-5696

Scenic Waterways
Parks and Recreation Div.
State of Oregon
525 Trade St. SE, Suite 301
Salem, Oregon 97310
(503)

Fish and Wildlife
Dept. of Fish and Wildlife
State of Oregon
5286 Table Rock Road
Central Point, Oregon 97502
(503) 776-6170

Safety
State Marine Board
State of Oregon
Administrative Office
3000 Market St. NW No. 505
Salem, Oregon 97310-0650
(503) 378-8587

Parks
Parks Department
Josephine County
101 NW A Street
Grants Pass, Oregon 97526
(503) 474-5285

Land Use
Planning Department
Josephine County
510 NW 4th
Grants Pass, Oregon 97526
(503) 474-5421

Removal or Filling of Materials
Division of State Lands
State of Oregon
1445 State Lands
Salem, Oregon 97310
(503) 378-3059

Safety
Sheriff's Office
Josephine County
Justice Building
Grants Pass, Oregon 97526
(503) 474-5120

III. GUIDES/RENTAL EQUIPMENT

The following guides offer services and/or rental equipment for the Hog run. They are located on the Merlin-Galice Road (from the Merlin Interstate (I-5) highway interchange to Grave Creek).

Galice Resort and Store
11744 Galice Rd.
Merlin, Oregon 97532
(503) 476-3818

Kingfisher, Ltd.
P.O. Box 107
Merlin, Oregon 97532.
(503) 479-1468

Merlin Sporting Goods
300 Merlin Rd.
Merlin, Oregon 97532.
(503) 476-6457

Morrison's Lodge
8500 Galice Rd.
Merlin, Oregon 97532.
(503) 476-3825

Otter River Trips
P.O. Box 338
Merlin, Oregon 97532.
(503) 476-8590

Paul Brooks Raft Trips
P.O. Box 638
Merlin, Oregon 97532.
(503) 476-8051

River Adventure Float Trips
2407 Merlin Rd.
Grants Pass, Oregon 97526.
(503) 476-6493

Rogue Canyon Guide Service
3388 Galice Rd.
Grants Pass, Oregon 97526.
(503) 479-9554

Rogue Wilderness Inc.
3388 Galice Rd.
Grants Pass, Oregon 97526.
(503) 479-9554

Sundance Expeditions Inc.
14894 Galice Rd.
Merlin, Oregon 97532.
(503) 479-8508

White Water Cowboys
209 Merlin Rd.
Merlin, Oregon 97532.
(503) 479-0132

Wilderness World Inc.
3388 Merlin Rd.
Merlin, Oregon 97532.
(503) 474-5545

By Michael L. Walker

APPENDIX B

INTERNATIONAL SCALE OF RIVER DIFFICULTY[1]

The international scale of river difficulty has six classes of riffles and/or rapids which are classified by individual river characteristics. Every riffle on the Hog Creek float is Class I or II on the international scale. This handbook identifies a refinement within this classification with a rating down to one-tenth of a class. The 25 identified riffles on the Hog Creek float have been assigned a difficulty class rating from 0.5 to 2.2 (see Table 6). If the water temperature is below 50 degrees fahrenheit the riffles should be considered one class more difficult (see Table 11).

CLASS I. Practiced Beginner - Moving water, sand banks, bends without difficulty, occasional small riffles with waves regular and low. Correct course easy to find, care necessary with minor or no obstacles.

CLASS II. Intermediate - Easy riffles with waves up to three feet, easy eddies, easy bends, and wide, clear, channels that are obvious with scouting. Some maneuvering is required.

CLASS III. Experienced - Maneuvering in rapids necessary. Small falls, high irregular waves often capable of swamping an open canoe. Narrow passages that often require complex maneuvering. Course not always recognizable, generally the limit of navigability for an expert in an open canoe. May require scouting from shore.

CLASS IV. Highly Skilled With Several Years Experience With Organized Groups - Large, rocky, rapids with difficult, completely irregular broken water which must be run head on. Very fast eddies, abrupt bends, and vigorous cross currents that often require precise maneuvering. Scouting from shore is often necessary, and conditions make rescue difficult. Generally not possible for open canoes.

CLASS V. Team of Experts - Extremely difficult, long and very violent rapids with highly congested routes which nearly always must be scouted from shore. Big drops, violent current, very steep gradient. Rescue conditions are difficult and there is significant hazard to life in event of a mishap.

CLASS VI. Teams of Experts - All previously mentioned difficulties increased to the limit. Nearly impossible and very dangerous. For teams of experts only after close study and with all precautions taken. Cannot be attempted without risk of life.

1. This river difficulty classification has been slightly modified from that identified in the State Marine Board brochure entitled, "Paddling Oregon Safety."

WHITE WATER INDEX

The white water index is a measure of the relative difficulty of the five identified river sections for the Hog Creek float as it relates to riffle difficulty class, riffle length (feet), and frequency of riffles in a river section. Its calculation is simple. Each riffle in a river section is identified. Each riffle's difficulty class is multiplied by its length in feet with the results totaled up and divided by the length of the river section in feet. For example, the Indian Mary Park to Ennis Boat Landing has a white water index of 0.2 as it is the easiest river section having only four short riffles all of which have a riffle difficulty class of less than Class I.

The following is the formula for calculating the white water index and the definitions of the formula symbols.

$$ WW = \frac{\sum_{i=1}^{n} (Y_1)(X_1) + ... + (Y_n)(X_n)}{L} $$

WWI = White Water Index
Y = Riffle Difficulty Class
X = Riffle Length (feet)
n = Number of Riffles in a River Section
L = Length of River Section in Feet

White Water Index	River Section
0.4 -	Hog Creek Boat Landing to Indian Mary Park Boat Landing
0.2 -	Indian Mary Park Boat Landing to Ennis Riffle Boat Landing
0.7 -	Ennis Riffle Boat Landing to Galice Store Boat Landing
0.4 -	Galice Store Boat Landing to Almeda Park Boat Landing
0.5 -	Almeda Park Boat Landing to Grave Creek Boat Landing

By Michael L. Walker

APPENDIX C
RIFFLE DIAGRAMS[1] 🐾

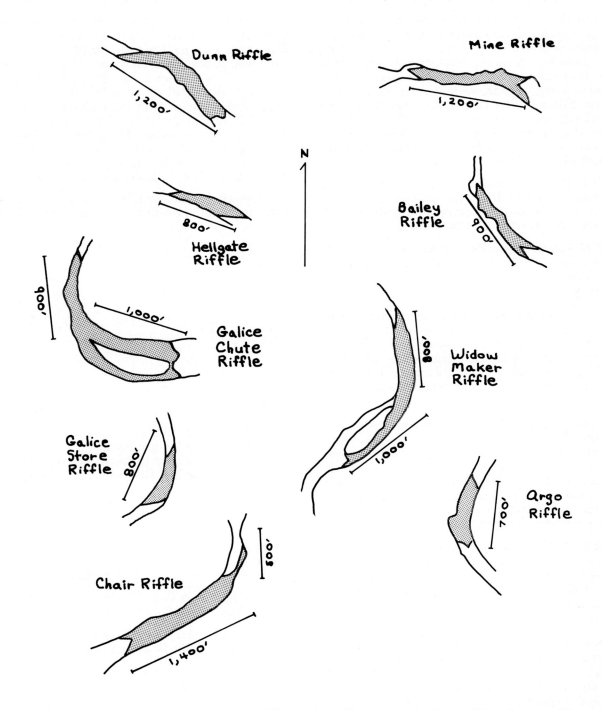

1. These nine riffles are on the Rogue River between Hog Creek and Grave Creek (see Table 6). The riffle diagrams were developed using 1985 color aerial photographs.

By Michael L. Walker

APPENDIX D
FLOATING SAFETY

Each part of the river is unique. Each riffle has its own stream action. Do you the floater understand whitewater? Is it exciting or is it dangerous? Would you float if the possibility of dying existed?

I. ATTITUDE AND PHYSICAL FITNESS

It is recommended that no young children float this section of the river unless under adult supervision. The adult floater does not have to be in great shape, but should be physically fit. The most important characteristic to possess is respect for the river without fear. This concept is similar to riding a motorcycle--it is not if you will crash, but when. Our water analogy is not if you will flip or fall out of your craft, but when. Part of the fun, when you have to, is the free float.

II. LIFE VESTS

All inflatables and rafts must carry a United States Coast Guard approved personal flotation device (PFD) for each person aboard. I do not know of anyone who has lost their life on the Hog Creek to Grave Creek stretch of the Rogue River when they were wearing their life vest. There are many instances where loss of life has occurred when the floater was not wearing a life vest (see Table 8; definition of PFD in glossary). It is only common sense that everyone wear their life vest whenever floating. Coast Guard approved PFDs that are not suitable for white water are the "horse collar" type life jackets and flotation seat cushions.

III. FOOT GEAR

Protective footgear is another necessity. Old tennis shoes work well. They protect your feet from glass, sharp rocks, and other objects onshore and in the river. If you go overboard in whitewater, and are in the proper position, shoes will also protect your body from hitting rocks.

IV. OTHER EQUIPMENT

Paddles, first-aid equipment, dry bags, food, sun screen, hat, and clothes (depending on your goals) are recommended equipment. The floater should bring no glass containers.

V. INFLATABLES AND DUCKIES

Inflatable kayaks have different handling characteristics than small paddle rafts (duckies), but they do have some things in common. They capsize if you are not in control. The too-casual attitude, or overloaded craft could put you into the water. Check your craft prior to put-in for its floatability.

VI. IN THE WATER

If your float is interrupted by a capsize, stay on the upriver side of the craft. This prevents the possibility of your being pinned against rocks or other obstacles by the craft. Try to get back into the inflatable quickly. If this is not possible, float downriver feet first. Your feet in tennis shoes will enable you to fend off rocks and other obstacles.

VII. KNOW YOUR WATER

A. Skills
Most accidents occur when floaters attempt water more demanding than their skills (see Appendix B).

B. Flow
The technical information explained in this guide is generally good from 1,900 cubic feet per second (cfs) to 2,200 cfs. The water classifications and "how to" will change with the water level. Check the flow before you go.

C. Water and Air Temperature
Maximum water temperatures out of Lost Creek Dam are cold, generally between 54 degrees F (fahrenheit) and 58 degrees F during the summer (see Table 11). Recommended minimum air temperatures without a wet-suit at these summer water temperatures are: 80 to 85 degrees F for inflatable kayakers and 75 to 80 degrees F for paddle rafters.

VIII. ALCOHOL

"Operating a boat is at least as complicated as driving a car and a boating accident can be just as dangerous as an automobile accident. Yet many people who would never drive drunk think it's safe to operate their boat after drinking. It isn't..."(State Marine Board).

IX. GROUPS

Never float alone. Group floats are fun and provide safety in numbers.

X. OBSTACLES

Always watch for rocks. **Read the river ahead.** Be especially aware of fallen trees, roots, bridge pilings, wire, fences, or anything which can become a strainer and hold you.

XI. FLOAT PLAN

At a minimum let someone know where you are going and when you plan on being home.

By Michael L. Walker

APPENDIX E
FLOATER SURVEY

By completing this survey and mailing it back to White Water Flips, you will:
  * Be notified of future editions.
  * Give us your ideas for improving and expanding this handbook.
  * Be entered into a lottery for a free one day Hog Creek float trip for a party of six in 1990. Lottery ends December, 1989.

Name: _____

Address: _____

_____   Date:_____

_____   Phone:_____

What are your objectives in visiting this section of the Rogue River?
☐ 1. Enjoying the natural beauty   ☐ 6. Using the developed parks
☐ 2. Floating/rafting trips   ☐ 7. Fishing
☐ 3. Recreational gold mining   ☐ 8. Jet boat rides
☐ 4. Wildlife viewing   ☐ 9. Plant viewing
☐ 5. Exploring cultural sites   ☐ 10. Other

Floats taken annually on Hog Creek Float?   ☐ 0   ☐ 1   ☐ 2 to 5   ☐ more than 5

Your Normal Put-in?   ☐ Hog Creek   ☐ Indian Mary   ☐ Ennis
       ☐ Galice   ☐ Almeda

Type of Craft Normally Floating In?   ☐ Inflatable   ☐ Paddle Raft
       ☐ Oar Raft   ☐ Drift Boat   ☐ Inner-tube

Used Your Own Equipment?   ☐ Yes ☐ No

Number of People Normally in Your Party?   _____ Number

Which Riffle(s) do You Like Best? _____

How Many Times do You Flip per Float (average)?   _____ Number

Have You Ever Wished You'd Had Your Life Vest on?   ☐ Yes ☐ No

Other comments or suggestions on this handbook:

_____

_____

_____

_____

_____

_____

_____

    By Michael L. Walker

APPENDIX F
BIBLIOGRAPHY

Alexander; Kraus; Kroll; Moffatt; and Smith. *Water Resources Data, Oregon, Water Year 1985* Vol. 2 Western Oregon. U.S. Geological Survey Water-Data Report OR-85-2. Portland: U.S. Geological Survey, 1987.

Arman, Florence. *The Rogue: A River To Run.* Grants Pass: Wildwood Press, 1982.

Armstead, Georgia and Schultz, Carolyn. *Mineral Wealth.* Southern Oregon Edition, 1904.

Atwood, Kay. *Josephine County Historical Resources Inventory, 1983 - 1984.* Volumes I and II. Grants Pass: Josephine County Planning Office, 1984.

Beckham, Stephen Dow. *Requiem For a People.* Norman: University of Oklahoma Press, 1971.

Booth, Percy T. *Legend of Indian Mary.* Grants Pass: Josephine County Historical Society, 1975.

Booth, Percy T. *Valley of the Rogues.* Grants Pass: Josephine County Historical Society, 1970.

Brooks, Howard, and Ramp, Len. *Gold and Silver in Oregon.* Bulletin 61. Portland: State of Oregon Department of Geology and Mineral Industries, 1968.

Diller, J. S. *Mineral Resources of Southwestern Oregon.* 1914.

Friday, John and Miller, Suzanne. *Statistical Summaries of Streamflow Data In Oregon, Volume 2. Western Oregon.* Open-file Report 84-454. Portland: U.S. Geological Survey, 1984.

Grants Pass Courier. *Golden Anniversary Edition.* Grants Pass: Grants Pass Courier, 1935.

Grants Pass Courier. *Diamond Anniversary Edition.* Grants Pass: Grants Pass Courier, 1960.

Harrison, Hal H. *A Field Guide to Western Birds' Nests.* Boston: Houghton Mifflen Company, 1979.

Heckert, Elizabeth. *The People and the River.* Ashland: Aquarius Press. 1977.

Hill, Edna May. *Josephine County Historical Highlights I.* Vol. 1. Grants Pass: Josephine County Library System and Josephine County Historical Society, 1976.

Hill, Edna May. *Josephine County Historical Highlights II.* Vol. 2. Grants Pass: Josephine County Library System, 1979.

Hydrology Subcommittee Columbia Basin Inter-agency Committee. *River Mile Index Rogue River, Pacific Slope Basin.* 1967.

Kent, William Eugene. *The Siletz Indian Reservation 1855 - 1900.* Portland: Portland State University, 1973.

Libbey, F. W. *The Almeda Mine - Josephine County, Oregon.*

McGinnis, William. *Whitewater Rafting.* New York and Toronto: Times Books, 1975.

Murphy, Martha Arman. Editor. *A History of Josephine County, Oregon.* Grants Pass: The Josephine County Historical Society, 1988.

Oregon, State of Oregon Department of Geology and Mineral Industries. *Gold and Silver in Oregon.* Baker: The Record-Courier Printers, 1980.

Oregon, State of Oregon Department of Geology and Mineral Industries. *Josephine County, Oregon Metal Mines Handbook.* Portland: 1952.

Oregon, State of Oregon Department of Geology and Mineral Industries. *Oregon Metal Mines Handbook, Josephine County.* Bulletin No. 14-C. Portland: 1952.

Oregon, State of Oregon Department of Geology and Mineral Industries. *Skin Diving For Gold in Oregon.* Brochure. Portland.

Oregon, State Marine Board. *Boating Synopsis.* Brochure. Salem: 1988.

Oregon, State Marine Board. *Oregon Boating Basics, A Small Craft Primer.* Salem: Outdoor Empire Publishing, Inc., 1985.

Oregon, State Marine Board, *Oregon Boaters Handbook.* Salem: State Marine Board, 1987.

Oregon, State Marine Board. *Paddling Oregon Safely.* Brochure.

Oregon, State Marine Board. *Tips For Safe Boating, Alcohol & Water Safety.* Salem.

Oregon, State Water Resources Board. *Rogue Drainage Basin.* Map No. 15.8. Salem: 1970.

Oregon, State Water Resources Board. *Rogue River Basin.* Salem: 1959.

Quinn, James M.; Quinn, James W.; and King, James G. *Handbook of the Rogue River Canyon.* Medford: Commercial Printing Company, 1978.

Ramp, Len, and Peterson, Norman. *Geology and Mineral Resources of Josephine County, Oregon.* Bulletin 100. Portland: State of Oregon Department of Geology and Mineral Industries, 1979.

Sutton, Dorothy and Jack. *Indian Wars of the Rogue River.* Grants Pass: Josephine County Historical Society, 1969.

Sutton, Jack. *110 Years With Josephine: The History of Josephine County.* Medford: Klocker Printery, 1966.

Udvardy, Miklos D. F. *The Audubon Society Field Guide to North American Birds Western Region.* Sacramento: 1977.

U.S. Department of Agriculture (USDA), Forest Service; and U.S. Department of Interior (USDI), Bureau of Land Management. *Black Bear.* Brochure. Medford.

U.S. Department of Agriculture (USDA),Siskiyou National Forest. *Historical Information, Galice Ranger District.*

U.S. Department of Agriculture (USDA), Forest Service; and U.S. Department of Interior (USDI), Bureau of Land Management. *Indians.* Brochure. Medford.

U.S. Department of Agriculture (USDA), Forest Service; and U.S. Department of Interior (USDI), Bureau of Land Management. *River Ethics.* Brochure. Medford.

U.S. Department of Agriculture (USDA), Forest Service; and U.S. Department of Interior (USDI), Bureau of Land Management. *River Otter.* Brochure. Medford.

U.S. Department of Agriculture (USDA), Forest Service; and U.S. Department of Interior (USDI), Bureau of Land Management. *Rogue River Ranch.* Brochure. Medford.

U.S. Department of Agriculture (USDA), Forest Service; and U.S. Department of Interior (USDI), Bureau of Land Management. *Steelhead.* Brochure. Medford.

U.S. Department of Agriculture (USDA), Forest Service; and U.S. Department of Interior (USDI), Bureau of Land Management. *The Wild and Scenic Rogue River.* Map. GPO #798-069. Medford.

U.S. Department of Agriculture (USDA), Forest Service; and U.S. Department of Interior (USDI), Bureau of Land Management. *Whitewater.* Brochure. Medford.

U.S. Department of the Interior (USDI), Bureau of Land Management (BLM). Ross A. Youngblood, District Manager. *A Sampling of the Occupancy Trespass Problem Within the Medford District: Bureau of Land Management, Medford, Oregon.* Medford: BLM, 1961.

U.S. Department of Interior (USDI), Bureau of Land Management (BLM). *Management Framework Plan for the Josephine Sustained Yield Unit.* Medford: BLM, 1979.

U.S. Department of the Interior (USDI), Bureau of Land Management (BLM). *Federal Register.* "*Prohibited Acts in the Rogue National Wild and Scenic River Area.*" Vol. 46. No. 107. p. 29991. Thursday, June 4, 1981.

U.S. Department of the Interior (USDI), Bureau of Land Management (BLM). *Rogue National Wild & Scenic River "Activity Plan": Hellgate Recreation Section.* Medford: BLM, 1978.

U.S. Department of the Interior (USDI), Bureau of Land Management (BLM). *Rogue River Occupancy Problem.* Medford: BLM, 1965.

U.S. Department of the Interior (USDI), Geological Survey, Water Resources Division. *Expanded Rating Table, Rogue River at Grants Pass, Oregon.* March, 1985.

U.S. Geological Survey (USGS). *Galice, Oregon Topographic Map.* 15-minute series. 1946.

U.S. Geological Survey (USGS). *Open-file Report 84-454.*

U.S. Surveyor General's Office (USSGO). *Original Township Land Survey Map for T.35S., R.7W., Willamette Meridian, Oregon.* 1856.

U.S. Surveyor General's Office (USSGO). *Original Township Land Survey Map for T.34S., R.7W., Willamette Meridian, Oregon.* 1893.

U.S. Surveyor General's Office (USSGO). *Original Township Land Survey Map for T. 35S., R.8W., Willamette Meridian, Oregon.* 1917.

U.S. Surveyor General's Office (USSGO). *Original Township Land Survey Map for T. 34S., R.8.W., Willamette Meridian, Oregon.* 1919.

U.S. Surveyor-General, Oregon. *Mineral Survey Number 734.* Dean Placer Claim. Portland: 1913.

U.S. Surveyor-General, Oregon. *Mineral Survey Number 796.* Grubstake Lode. 1917.

Wade, Edward C. Editor. *Oregon Mining Journal.* Grants Pass: Oregon Mining Journal Publishing Company, 1897.

Walsh, Frank K. *Indian Battles Along the Rogue River 1855-56.* Te-Cum-Tom Pub. 1972.

APPENDIX G
GLOSSARY

The following definitions are generic as well as specific to this section of the Rogue River.

Aboard - On, in, or into a boat.

Afloat - On the water.

Amidships - Center of vessel with reference to its length and/or sometimes its width.

Aft - Toward the stern, back, or tail of a vessel.

Bail - To remove water from a boat by pump or bailer.

Bar - A ridge of sand, gravel, or other material deposited by the river.

Beam - The boat's/vessel's maximum width.

Big Water - Where massive waves, powerful currents, and large holes are obstacles (rather than rocks).

BLM/Forest Service Information Center (🏠) - A government information center at Rand, Oregon where information, maps, and float permits for the wild section of the Rogue are obtained.

Blue Heron Rookery (△) - The location of a colony of Blue Herons. This place is where the gregarious heron congregates and breeds.

Boat Landing (●) - 1. A place where boats are put-in or taken-out from the river, usually from paved or concrete roads; 2. Place to put-in or take-out, get in line, meet new friends, the beginning or the end.

Boat/Vessel - Every description of watercraft used or capable of being used as a means of transportation on the water, but does not include aircraft equipped to land on water, boathouses, floating homes, air mattresses, beach and water toys, or single innertubes.

Bodysurfing - A person riding the crest of standing waves.

Bow - Forward part of a vessel.

Bracing - A maneuver by which a kayaker or inflatable kayaker steadies his boat with a paddle to prevent a flip (see river mile 14.1, Sloppy Nostalgia).

Bureau of Land Management (BLM) Recreation Site (▼) - Sites managed by the BLM for recreational purposes.

Chevy Pickup (1941) - Exciting chariot to the adult world.

Choppy Water - River water which is forming irregular, short, broken, waves.

Chute - A place on the river where the channel narrows and the gradient of the river bottom is steep.

Cubic Feet Per Second (cfs) - A scientific standard used to measure the amount of water (vs. feet) passing a particular point on the river in one second.

Cushion - The layer of slack or billowing water that pads the upriver face of rocks and other obstacles.

Day-use Area (✗) - A site where outdoor activities are conducted during the day time. Camping is prohibited in a day-use area.

Difficulty Class Rating - See international scale of river difficulty.

Disneyland Float - See Hog Run.

Downriver - A perspective of looking or floating in the direction the river is flowing.

Drift Boat - A wooden or aluminum boat which has a raked bottom fore and aft, and flared sides. The design makes the boat ride high and maneuver well in white water. It is primarily used for fishing.

Dry Bag - A water-tight rubber container in which you keep your clothes and other personal items dry.

Dry Camp (△) - Dry camp sites commonly consist solely of a level site, and perhaps an old fire ring. They lack drinkable water and may lack toilet facilities. However, you can be assured of beautiful solitude and pleasant scenery.

Ducky - Inexpensive, small, inflatable kayak or paddle raft which is made of thin, light, material and is prone to puncturing and blowing up when hitting rocks.

Eddy (⟳) - A river current at variance with the main current, usually having a rotary or whirling motion. Eddies can be found on the downriver side of surface rocks.

Eighty-five Percent (85%) Solution - Life jackets are often referred to as the 85% solution to fatal boat accidents. In other words, 85% of all boating fatalities would have been prevented had the victim worn a life jacket.

Farmer-john - An armless wet-suit. It looks like a rubber, armless coverall. It helps keep you warm in chilly water.

Feet - A measurement standard used to indicate the amount of water in the Rogue River passing the Grants Pass Water Filtration Plant. It is a relative standard which does not indicate the amount of water, but the height of river as measured at the plant (see cubic feet per second).

Float Plan (minimum) - Before you go boating, tell someone--a relative or a friend--where you are going and when to expect you back.

Flip - The action when your boat capsizes after turning over on its bottom.

Float Time (🕐) - The time it takes to drift, float, or travel from one point to another on the river.

Freeboard - Height of vessel's side measured from waterline to deck or gunwale.

Gold Fever - The frantic need to seek and hoard gold.

Gravel Bar - See bar.

Gunwale - Top, outer, edge of boat's hull.

Heavy Duty Oar Raft - A 13 to 16 foot paddle raft with a frame for using large oars to move and maneuver. The raft is expensive and made of thick, heavy, durable, material.

Highside - If the raft is going to hit a rock broadside, the entire crew should immediately jump to the side of the raft nearest the rock or highside. This allows the upriver side of the raft to rise and the water to flow beneath. Going highside can help prevent a flip.

Higher Water Level - Greater than 3,000 cfs at Grants Pass, Oregon.

Historic Mine (⛏) - A historic placer or lode gold mine.

Historic Site (■) - This map symbol on Maps 2 through 9 usually indicates the site of a residence which used to be along the river. The use of the map symbol in the text indicates a event of historical significance other than Indian or mining history.

Hog Run - Wet, pleasurable, exhilarating white water float on the Rogue River from Hog Creek to Grave Creek involving friends, scenery, and solitude.

Hole (⊔) - Fast water falling over a boulder or ledge and plunging to or near the river bottom before turning downriver. The place where this fast current swings upward and revolves back on itself forming a meeting of the currents is called a hole, or reversal.

Hydraulic - A general term for reversals, eddies, shear zones, and other places where there is a current differential.

Hypothermia - A physical condition where the body loses heat faster than it can produce it, a dangerous situation.

Improved Campground (▲) - This kind of campground has a fee charge, paved access, toilets, and other amenities. They are frequented largely by tourists.

Indian History (⚒) - Indian history usually associated with the Rogue Indian War along the Rogue River from 1855 to 1856.

Inflatable Kayak - A one or two person boat which needs to be inflated with air to float. It averages about 12 feet long by 2 and 1/2 feet at the beam. The yellow Tahiti is the most popular.

Inflatable Kayaker - Someone other than a hard shell kayaker. A person interested in the pursuit of fun rather than demanding technique.

International Scale of River Difficulty - A scale of classifying the difficulty of white water on a scale of I through VI with Class I being the least difficult and Class VI being almost unfloatable (see Appendix B).

Jaws - Fictitious name to describe an entrance to excitement.

Jumping Rock (✕) - A rock from which you can jump or dive into the deep water of the Rogue. Always check for rocks under the water before jumping or diving.

Keeper - A keeper is a type of reversal or hole which has water moving upriver in a manner which keeps the craft caught in it.

Landing - See boat landing.

Left Bank - The land side of the river to the left/port when facing downriver.

Life Vest - Life vest and life jacket are used interchangeably. A life vest is one type of a personal floatation device (PFD) (see personal floatation device).

Life Jacket - See life vest; personal floatation device.

Low Flow - Less than 1,700 cfs at Grants Pass, Oregon.

Midriver - A point equidistant from the opposite banks of the river.

Oar Raft - A paddle raft of any size and material designed with a frame for oars (see heavy duty oar raft).

Paddle Raft - A raft without a frame. Propulsion is accomplished by paddles in the hands of each rafter. Size ranges from 12 feet long by 5 feet at the beam to lengths up to 16 feet.

Personal Floatation Device (PFD) - A PFD is a life jacket/life vest and is the most important safety device you can own. There are five types of PFDs. The most popular for this stretch are Type III and Type V. A Type III has a minimum of 15.5 pounds of buoyancy. The Type III is not designed to turn an unconscious victim to a vertical or slightly backward position. However, once a person assumes this position, this PFD will maintain it. A Type V has restricted USCG approval allowing it to be used in lieu of a Type I for white water activities. It is specifically designed for white water use. It provides a minimum buoyant force of 22 pounds. One PFD is required in your boat for each person aboard. Remember, no buoyant device of any kind has ever been a sure guarantee against drowning. PFDs provide BUOYANCY to support or "float" the wearer, but vigilance and safety-sense, plus a good buoyant device are the surest protections. WEAR IT...DON'T STOW IT!

Pennyweight - Twenty troy pennywights is equal to one troy ounce which is the basic unit of weight used in dealing with gold. In the jewelry industry, the common unit of measurement is the pennyweight which is equivalent to 1.555 grams.

Placer Deposit - A concentration of gold derived from lode deposits by erosion, disintegration or decomposition of the enclosing rock, and subsequent concentration by gravity.

Put-in - Usually a boat landing which is the start of your float trip.

Port - Side of vessel to the left when facing forward or toward the bow.

Osprey Nest (◯) - The location of the nest of an Osprey, usually located on the top of a Douglas Fir snag with a broken top.

Read the River Ahead - Paddlers need to know how to read the river. Where are the rocks, reversals, shear zones, and "V's"? For instance, upriver "V's" indicate rocks. Downriver "V's" with large stationary waves indicate gaps between rocks.

Reckless Operation; Speed - A person commits the crime of reckless operation of a boat when he or she operates a boat carelessly and heedlessly in willful or wanton disregard of the rights, safety, or property of others. No person shall operate any boat at a rate of speed greater than that which will permit that person in the exercise of reasonable care to bring the boat to a stop within the assured clear distance ahead.

Recreation Corridor Boundary (▨) - The legal boundary of the National Wild and Scenic Rogue River for the Hog Creek float. It averages a quarter mile inland from both banks of the river (see Map 2).

Reversal (⊔⊔) - A place where a fast current swings upward on itself forming a meeting of the currents after passing over a rock or ledge (see hole).

Right Bank - The land side of the river to the right/starboard when facing downriver.

River Bar - See bar.

Riffle (〰) - White water with a difficulty class rating of I or II (see international scale of river difficulty).

Riffle Class - The difficulty rating of a group of riffles with similar characteristics (see international scale of river difficulty).

Rock (⬭) - A visible rock in the channel of the river which is above the surface of the water.

Rock Garden - Many rocks in the river which require maneuvering around as you float downriver.

Rock Side - See high side.

Rules of the Road - The nautical traffic rules for preventing collisions on the water. For example, normally a non-powered boat has the right-of-way. In essence, this means a power-driven craft must yield to a non-powered craft, however, the non-powered boat must (given the opportunity to do so) make passage for the powered vessel.

Sandpaper - Small choppy waves over shallows.

Scouting - Plan your approach in advance when approaching unknown riffles or obstructions. If in doubt, determine your float route by scouting from shore. The information received may influence you to portage.

Shallows - An area of the river where the water depth is shallow to the point where your boat may touch the bottom.

Shear Zone - A place in the river where there is a strong difference in the flow of adjacent currents.

Shuttle Rig - A vehicle which is left at the take-out for the purpose of hauling rafters and their gear back upriver to the put-in or home.

By Michael L. Walker

Sleeper Rock - A rock in the river which is not visible as it is slightly below the surface of the water.

Sloppy Nostalgia - Silly memories of the author's float trips on the Hog Run of the Rogue River. This is usually about the author's family or friends. The sloppy nostalgia text sections are true, but are characteristically frivolous and different than the technical and historical sections.

Small Water - A stretch of the river with a riffle difficulty of less than a Class 0.5.

Socioeconomic Background - A mouthful: some academician's view of how to classify people.

Squeeze Test - When you are trying to figure out how much air to put in your paddle raft or inflatable you squeeze the tubes with your hand. The tube must be taut, but not so hard it could blow up in the hot sun as the air expands.

Standing Wave (⌒⌒) - A wave caused by the deceleration of a current that occurs when fast moving water slams into slower moving water.

Starboard - Side of vessel to right when facing forward or toward the bow of the boat.

Stern - The stern is toward the back, tail, or aft end of a vessel.

Strainer - Brush, fallen trees, bridge pilings, or anything else that allows the current to sweep through, but pins boats and boaters. These are lethal.

Swift Water - Water traveling fast enough to make it difficult to impossible for a person to walk on the river bottom unaided.

Tahiti - A yellow inexpensive inflatable kayak produced by Sevylor.

Take-out - Usually a boat landing which is the end of your float trip.

Thin-skinned - Small inexpensive paddle rafts or inflatable kayaks which are light weight and are made of thin material.

Tongue or "V" (/\ ) - Sometimes called the apron, the largest "V" shaped tongue of smooth water above a riffle or rapid marks the path of the main current, and is usually the best and safest point of entry for boats.

Underway - Vessel in motion. Technically a vessel is underway when not moored, at anchor or aground.

Upriver - A perspective of looking or boating in the opposite direction the river is flowing.

Unsafe Operation - A person commits a crime of unsafe operation of a boat if the person operates a boat in a manner that endangers or would be likely to endanger any person or property.

"V" (/\ ) - See tongue.

White Water Index - A measurement of the intensity of white water action on a particular stretch of the river (see Appendix B).

Wrap - When a raft or inflatable kayak is pinned flat or bent around a rock or other obstruction by the current.

APPENDIX H
RIVER MILEPOST

HOG CREEK BOAT LANDING TO INDIAN MARY PARK BOAT LANDING

0.0 River Mile, Hog Creek Boat Landing
0.1 River Mile, Hog Riffle
0.2 River Mile, Hellgate Canyon
0.5 River Mile, Hellgate Canyon Overlook
0.7 River Mile, Dunn Riffle
1.2 River Mile, Hellgate Riffle
1.4 River Mile, Bridge Riffle
1.4 River Mile, Hellgate Bridge
1.7 River Mile, Stratton Creek
   Recreation Site

INDIAN MARY PARK BOAT LANDING TO ENNIS RIFFLE BOAT LANDING

2.5 River Mile, Indian Mary Park
   Boat Landing
2.6 River Mile, Indian Riffle
2.9 River Mile, Rainbow Recreation Site
3.0 River Mile, Massie Riffle
3.1 River Mile, Taylor Creek Gorge
3.4 River Mile, Morrison Lodge
   River Bend/Taylor Creek
3.5 River Mile, Taylor Creek Riffle
3.8 River Mile, Old Man Riffle
3.9 River Mile, Ennis Flat Water

ENNIS RIFFLE BOAT LANDING TO GALICE STORE BOAT LANDING

4.7 River Mile, Ennis Riffle Boat Landing
4.8 River Mile, Ennis Riffle
4.9 River Mile, Carpenter's Island
   Flat Water
5.7 River Mile, Carpenter's Island
5.7 River Mile, Galice Chute Riffle
5.8 River Mile, Carpenter's Island
   Recreation Site
6.0 River Mile, Historic Galice Creek
6.6 River Mile, Galice Store Riffle

GALICE STORE BOAT LANDING TO ALMEDA PARK BOAT LANDING

6.8 River Mile, Galice Store Boat Landing
7.1 River Mile, Rocky Riffle
7.2 River Mile, Rocky Riffle Area
7.3 River Mile, Twin Rocks Riffle
8.1 River Mile, Red Rock Cut-Bank
8.3 River Mile, Garden Riffle
8.3 River Mile, Historic Robert Dean
   Placer Mine
8.9 River Mile, Chair Riffle
8.9 River Mile, Chair Recreation Site
9.1 River Mile, Rand Recreation Site
   Boat Ramp
9.1 River Mile, Ash Gulch
9.3 River Mile, Rand Visitors Center
9.7 River Mile, Widow Maker
   (Mark's) Riffle

ALMEDA BOAT LANDING TO GRAVE CREEK BOAT LANDING

10.0 River Mile, Almeda Park Boat Landing
10.3 River Mile, Mine Riffle
10.3 River Mile, Almeda Mine
10.9 River Mile, Bailey Riffle
11.0 River Mile, Bailey Canyon
11.7 River Mile, Argo Riffle
11.9 River Mile, Sizemore's Bar Riffle
12.2 River Mile, Argo Landing
12.2 River Mile, Argo Landing Riffle
12.3 River Mile, Canyon Riffle
12.5 River Mile, Argo Canyon
12.7 River Mile, Smith Gulch Riffle
13.0 River Mile, No Name Riffle
13.5 River Mile, Wooldridge Riffle
14.0 River Mile, Grave Creek Bridge
14.1 River Mile, Grave Creek Boat Landing